First World War
and Army of Occupation
War Diary
France, Belgium and Germany

52 DIVISION
Divisional Troops
9 Brigade Royal Field Artillery
1 April 1918 - 30 April 1919

WO95/2892/2

The Naval & Military Press Ltd
www.nmarchive.com
Published in association with The National Archives

Published by

The Naval & Military Press Ltd

Unit 10 Ridgewood Industrial Park,

Uckfield, East Sussex,

TN22 5QE England

Tel: +44 (0) 1825 749494

www.naval-military-press.com

www.nmarchive.com

This diary has been reprinted in facsimile from the original. Any imperfections are inevitably reproduced and the quality may fall short of modern type and cartographic standards.

© Crown Copyright
Images reproduced by permission of The National Archives, London, England, 2015.

Contents

Document type	Place/Title	Date From	Date To
Heading	WO95/2892-2 9 Brigade Royal Field Artillery		
Heading	52nd Division 9th Brigade R.F.A. Apr 1918-Apr 1919 From Egypt 7 (Meerut) Division		
Heading	52nd Divisional Artillery Disembarked Marseilles From Egypt 12.4.18 9th Brigade R.F.A. April 1918 Torpedoed 11.4.18		
War Diary	Ismailia (Moascar Camp)	01/04/1918	02/04/1918
War Diary	Alexandria Docks	03/04/1918	03/04/1918
War Diary	At Sea	04/04/1918	11/04/1918
War Diary	Marseilles	12/04/1918	12/04/1918
War Diary	France	14/04/1918	14/04/1918
War Diary	Grand Laviers	17/04/1918	26/04/1918
War Diary	Bealcourt	27/04/1918	27/04/1918
War Diary	Linzeux	28/04/1918	28/04/1918
War Diary	Crequy	29/04/1918	29/04/1918
Heading	War Diary Of 9th Brigade Royal Field Artillery From 1st May 1918 To 31st May 1918		
War Diary	Grand	23/04/1918	23/04/1918
War Diary	Laviers	23/04/1918	26/04/1918
War Diary	Bealcourt	27/04/1918	27/04/1918
War Diary	Linzeux	28/04/1918	28/04/1918
War Diary	Crequy	29/04/1918	12/05/1918
War Diary	Wavrans	12/05/1918	12/05/1918
War Diary	Tinques	15/05/1918	15/05/1918
War Diary	Le Pendu	16/05/1918	27/05/1918
War Diary	Vimy	28/05/1918	31/05/1918
Heading	War Diary Of 9th Brigade Royal Field Artillery From 1st To 30th June 1918 Volume 6/1918		
War Diary	Vimy	01/06/1918	29/06/1918
Miscellaneous	Increases and Decreases in Personnel for Month of June 1918		
Heading	War Diary Of 9th Brigade Royal Field Artillery From 1st To 31st July 1918 Volume 7/1918		
War Diary	Vimy	01/07/1918	21/07/1918
War Diary	Hermin	22/07/1918	23/07/1918
War Diary	Madagascar Camp	24/07/1918	24/07/1918
War Diary	Hermin Pas-De-Calais	25/07/1918	28/07/1918
War Diary	Madagascar Camp	29/07/1918	29/07/1918
War Diary	North Of R. Scarpe NE. Of Arras HQ At H F.A.1.2	30/07/1918	31/07/1918
Miscellaneous	Increase & Decrease In Personnel For Month Of July 1918		
Heading	War Diary Of 9th Brigade Royal Field Artillery From 1st Aug To 31st August 1918 Volume 8/1918		
War Diary	NE. Of Arras H.7.a.1.2	01/08/1918	05/08/1918
War Diary	H.1.C.70.65 (Maroevil Map)	06/08/1918	07/08/1918
War Diary	Roclincourt	08/08/1918	17/08/1918
War Diary	Acq	18/08/1918	21/08/1918
War Diary	Beaumetz	22/08/1918	22/08/1918
War Diary	Near Ficheux	23/05/1918	24/05/1918
War Diary	Near Mercatel	25/05/1918	30/08/1918

War Diary	Fontaine-Lez Croisilles	31/08/1918	31/08/1918
Heading	War Diary Of 9th Brigade Royal Field Artillery From 1st To 30th September 1918 Volume 9/1918		
War Diary	Fontaine-Lez-Croisilles	01/09/1918	01/09/1918
War Diary	Cagnicourt	02/09/1918	02/09/1918
War Diary	Pronville	03/09/1918	05/09/1918
War Diary	Near Pronville	06/09/1918	09/09/1918
War Diary	Pronville	10/09/1918	19/09/1918
War Diary	Boursies	20/09/1918	26/09/1918
War Diary	E Of Moeuvres	27/09/1918	27/09/1918
War Diary	Cantaing	28/09/1918	30/09/1918
Miscellaneous	Increase And Decrease For Month Of September 1918	01/10/1918	01/10/1918
War Diary	Cantaing	01/10/1918	05/10/1918
War Diary	N.E. Of Noyelles Near Escaut	06/10/1918	07/10/1918
War Diary	N. Noyelles	08/10/1918	08/10/1918
War Diary	S Of Cambrai	09/10/1918	09/10/1918
War Diary	Nr Rieux	10/10/1918	11/10/1918
War Diary	St Aubert	12/10/1918	17/10/1918
War Diary	Proville Nr Cambrai	18/10/1918	19/10/1918
War Diary	Morchies	20/10/1918	20/10/1918
War Diary	Ecurie	21/10/1918	23/10/1918
War Diary	Courcelles Les-Lens	24/10/1918	26/10/1918
War Diary	Waziers	27/10/1918	31/10/1918
Heading	War Diary Of 9th Brigade R.F.A. From 1/11/18 To 30/11/18 Volume 8		
War Diary	Waziers	01/11/1918	04/11/1918
War Diary	Nivelle	05/11/1918	08/11/1918
War Diary	Harchies	09/11/1918	09/11/1918
War Diary	Vacresse	10/11/1918	30/11/1918
War Diary	Waziers	01/11/1918	04/11/1918
War Diary	Nivelle	05/11/1918	08/11/1918
War Diary	Harchies	09/11/1918	09/11/1918
War Diary	Har Vacresse	10/11/1918	30/11/1918
Heading	War Diary Of 9th Brigade R.F.A. From 1/12/18 To 31/12/18 (Volume 12)		
War Diary	Vacresse	01/12/1918	11/12/1918
War Diary	Casteau	12/12/1918	31/12/1918
Heading	War Diary 9th Brigade R.F.A. From 1st January 1919 To 31st January 1919 Vol I/1919		
War Diary	Casteau Belgium 10 Kilos N. Of Mons	01/01/1919	07/01/1919
War Diary	Casteau	08/01/1919	31/01/1919
Heading	War Diary Of 9th Brigade R.F.A. From 1/2/19 To 28/2/19 (Volume 2)		
War Diary	Casteau	01/02/1919	28/02/1919
Heading	War Diary Of 9th Brigade R.F.A. From 1/3/19 To 31/3/19 (Volume 3)		
War Diary	Casteau	02/03/1919	20/03/1919
War Diary	Soignies	21/03/1919	31/03/1919
Heading	War Diary Of 9th Brigade R.F.A. From 1/4/19 To 30/4/19 (Volume 4)		
War Diary	Soignies	10/04/1919	30/04/1919

WO95/2892/2

9 Brigade Royal Field Artillery

52ND DIVISION

9TH BRIGADE R.F.A.
APR 1918-APR 1919

~~FROM MESOPOTAMIA~~
~~VIA EGYPT~~

FROM EGYPT 7 (MEERUT) DIVISION

52nd Divisional Artillery.
———————

Disembarked MARSEILLES from EGYPT 12.4.18.

9th BRIGADE R. F. A.

APRIL 1918.

Torpedoed 11.4.18.

Army Form C. 2118.

WAR DIARY
or
INTELLIGENCE SUMMARY.   9th Brigade R.F.A

(Erase heading not required.)

Place	Date 1918	Hour	Summary of Events and Information	Remarks and references to Appendices
ISMAILIA (MOASCAR CAMP)	1.4		Orders for move to ALEXANDRIA. All horses handed into Remounts & all harness to Ordnance.	A/2
"	2.4		Entrained at MOASCAR; first train left at 9.21 p.m.	A/2
ALEXANDRIA DOCKS	3.4		Arrived about 5 a.m. & embarked on H.T. KINGSTONIAN, together with HQ, Divn D.A.C., & 41st Bgde R.F.A.	A/2
At Sea	6.4		Sailed at 4.30 p.m. in a convoy of 26 ships including escort.	A/2
"	10.4		H.T. WARWICKSHIRE torpedoed about 6.30 a.m. 82 miles from BIZERTA	A/2
"	11.4		H.T. KINGSTONIAN torpedoed West of SARDINIA at 5.32 a.m. Troops transhipped to H.M.S. LYCHNIS, who came alongside. Some of the men who were cut away in the ship's boats were picked up by H.M.S. BERBERIS. Gnrs JAMES & D. PHILLIPS killed by explosion. 2 B.O.Rs. H.T. KINGSTONIAN taken in tow 6 B.O.Rs missing, presumed by explosion 2 B.O.Rs. H.T. KINGSTONIAN beached in coast of SARDINIA. Lieut MARTIN and by H.M.S. BERBERIS, & eventually 35 B.O.Rs. left aboard to guard kit.	A/2
MARSEILLES	12.4		Arrived early morning, disembarked, & after being fitted with necessary clothing, marched to No 2 Camp	A/3

Army Form C. 2118.

WAR DIARY
or
INTELLIGENCE SUMMARY.
(Erase heading not required.)

Place	Date 1918	Hour	Summary of Events and Information	Remarks and references to Appendices
FRANCE	14.4		Entrained at MARSEILLES at 8.30 A.m. & left at 10 A.m.	
GRAND LAVIERS	17.4		Arrived ABBEVILLE Station 8 a.m. & marched to billets, no wagons guns, wagons, horses or transport.	
			H.Q.	
			Maj A.B. LOCK D.S.O.	
			2/Lt C. KERRIDGE (adjt)	
			Lt. H.E. STANLEY (O.O)	
			Capt A. ROBB R.A.M.C. (M.O)	
			Lt Col. MEIKLE, Appointed Hon. Colonel (attached)	
			Rev HEWITT A.C.D (attached)	
			14 B.y	
			Maj N.M. ADAM	
			Capt V.S. LONGMAN	
			Lieut T.M. SWALES	
			2/Lt R.H. ENGLEFIELD	
			2/Lt A.R.H. MALCOLM	
			20 B.y	
			2/Capt J. BOYD	
			Lieut M.J. deKOCK	
			Lieut E.A.T. HAWKE	
			Lieut W.A. WOLLACOTT	
			2/Lt L.W. JUDD	A/13
			28 B.y	6/13
			Maj S.P. BURNE D.S.O	
			2/Capt A.W. SMYTHE	
			Lt E.W. ALTREE	
			Lt T. BECKER	
			2/Lt M. MEABURN	
			3/67 B.y	
			Capt J.P. HICKEY	
			Capt H.A.N. WALSHE	
			Lt D.M. UPSON	
			Lt A.T.W. ROWELL	
			Lt C. MYERS	
			" WINSHIP	
	21.4		4 officers & 12 B.O.R.s to CALAIS to take over gun equipment	
	22.4		Commenced drawing horses from Ordnance	

Army Form C. 2118.

WAR DIARY
or
INTELLIGENCE SUMMARY.
(Erase heading not required.)

Instructions regarding War Diaries and Intelligence Summaries are contained in F. S. Regs., Part II and the Staff Manual respectively. Title pages will be prepared in manuscript.

Place	Date 1918	Hour	Summary of Events and Information	Remarks and references to Appendices
GRAND RULLERS	23 to 26.4		Guns & wagons from CALAIS. Horses from Remounts. Ammunition from SAIGNEVILLE.	Many stores still deficient
BEALCOURT	27.4	9.30am	Marched to billets here. 26 miles. Arrived 5.30pm. Watering facilities poor. Mgr ROOM, Lt MALCOLM, Lt HANKE, Lt WOOLLACOTT, Lt PITREE, Lt MEABURN, Lt POWELL, Lt MAYERS, left at T.G. School, SHILLY-LE-SEC on course.	
LINZEUX	28.4	10am	Marched to billets. 13 miles. Arrived 2pm. Watering facilities - bad.	
CREQUY	29.4	11.am	" " 15 miles. Arrived 5.30pm. Good watering facilities, but billets scattered	

A. Scott
Lieut.Col.R.A.
Comdg. 7 Brigade R.H.A.

Confidential   Original

War Diary

9 Brigade Royal Horse Artillery.

From 1st May 1915.
to 31st May 1918.

Volume 5/1918.

Army Form C. 2118.

WAR DIARY
or
INTELLIGENCE SUMMARY.
(Erase heading not required.)

Instructions regarding War Diaries and Intelligence Summaries are contained in F. S. Regs., Part II. and the Staff Manual respectively. Title pages will be prepared in manuscript.

Place	Date 1918	Hour	Summary of Events and Information	Remarks and references to Appendices
GARNID LAVIERS	23 to 26.4		Guns & wagons from CALAIS. Horses from remounts. Many stores slow difficult. Ammunition from SAIGNEVILLE.	A/3
BEAUCOURT	27.4	9.30 AM	Marched to billets there. 26 miles. Arrived 5.20 p.m. Watering facilities poor. Maj ADAM, Lt MALCOLM, Lt HAWKE, Lt WOLLACOTT, Lt ALTREE, Lt MEABURN, Lt POWELL, Lt MAYERS left at R.A. School, SAILLY-LE-SEC on course.	A/3
LINZEUX	28.4	10. AM	Marched to billets. 13 miles. Arrived 2 p.m. Watering facilities bad.	A/3
CREQUY	29.4	10. A.M	" 15 miles. Arrived 5:30 p.m. Good watering facilities but billets scattered.	A/3
"	30.4			A/3
"	1.5		H.H.Q.	A/3
"	2.5		Captain E.W. WALSHE. D/69 Battery appointed Adjutant vice that C. KERRIDGE posted to 19 Bg. R.F.A. Ordnance stores, including saddles & fitters tools arrived from CALAIS.	A/3
"	3.5		Now belong to XI Corps, 1st Army. Maj. BURNE, D.S.O., Capt BOYD, Lt ENGLEFIELD, Lt UPSON & 4 signallers for Battery to MOLINGHEM to study local artillery methods.	A/3
"	8.5		Fitters arrived from Ordnance. Fitters from 16th Batteries to PERNES for instruction in tank buffer. Marched to WAVRANS. 14 miles. Billets scattered & bad. Officers found & posted to Batteries as shown. Lt L. O. PARROT, 19 Bg., Lt K.J.C. ALISON, 20 Bg., 2 Lt A.J. ROSS & Lt R. HAWKES, 28 Bg., Lt A. ANDERSON. D/69 Bg.	A/3
"	12.5		Maj ADAM, Lt PARROT, Lt de ROCK, Lt JUDD, Lt ALTREE, Lt ROSS, Lt to XVIII Corps front for instruction. Also Capt. WALSHE, & 2 Lt REEVES, R.E. (Sig. Off.) & a party of N.C.O.'s. Gunn.	A/3

Army Form C. 2118.

WAR DIARY
or
INTELLIGENCE SUMMARY.
(Erase heading not required.)

Instructions regarding War Diaries and Intelligence Summaries are contained in F. S. Regs., Part II and the Staff Manual respectively. Title pages will be prepared in manuscript.

Place	Date	Hour	Summary of Events and Information	Remarks and references to Appendices
WAVRANS	12.5		Maj BURNE D.S.O. away on attachment to Cavalry staff for instruction. Capt BOYD & 2nd Lt MEABURN on leave to U.K.	W/D
	11.5		Leave opened at Rouen a day if for 14 days leave.	W/D
TINQUES	15.5	8.30 AM	marched to TINQUES 15 miles	
LE PENDU	16.5	8.40	" " 12	
	18.5		Capt LONGMAN on leave to U.K.	
	21.5	8.30	Lt Col OTTER C.M.G. D.S.O. returned, the BDE generally resting.	
	23.5	11.0	Maj BLACK D.S.O. on leave to U.K. Preparation for move open warfare commenced. Maj ADAM to hospital also Lt TINDALLS.	
	24.5		Lt Col Carter allots position for front line on very ridge. Day very wet. Orders received the brigade would relieve night of 25/26 orders subsequently altered to night 1/27/28 as very trench & horse shelling but more proper had been made on ridge. Camouflage material also very scarce.	DSO
	25.5		Orders received the brigade out & have own certain number of mules to 50 over R.M. of each reserve horses in exchange. The intention is that all firing batteries vehicles chance to horse. mules being used for first line wagons and transport. This arrangement will leave the brigade to one last leaves Hq 2 1/2 guns out & change to register. Lt Col OTTER selects O.P. on VIMY ridge to brigade.	DSO

Army Form C. 2118.

WAR DIARY
INTELLIGENCE SUMMARY.
(Erase heading not required.)

9th Brigade C.F.A.   May 1918.

Place	Date	Hour	Summary of Events and Information	Remarks and references to Appendices
LE PENDU	26/5 Sunday		Nothing to note. AHe	
	27/5		Considerable firing in the forward area early morning. Heavy H.V. fire which came near Bde H.Qrs. & from 8 a.m. & about gas fired sniped in vicinity of ammo dump on M.34.c.09 and t from 9.30. fired sniped with my left hand over Bde H.Qr. Posit. ranging by time burst. About 2.30pm N°70694 Dr. PAGE – 19/85 Bdr killed & 46904 G. BURROWS, 72390 Gbr HILL, and 57787 Gbr GREY 28/85 wounded from made 28/85 killed by an explosion in the lines, probably a bomb fire an aeroplane at 8-15pm Brigade line 28/85 moved up but retn to rest position in VIMY ROCK Gully in by about midnight. 28/85 are Artillery fire queer queein under SW 23/28 R94. g.Bde fire a outpost under the right group R.F.A. 62°Dr. AHe	
VIMY	28/5		Battn in action in the line. Off.P.S. Loc. and found having in FORBES's alley from D./52 battn. Heavy shelling vicinity of g.9.Bde H.Qrs. S.A. 8 hill. AHe	
	29/5		9/23 acting aspirator gun trans. Col. 15/69 finder gas so wrong to follow up telephone communication which has been very bad. AHe	
	30/5		20: LO/69 aspirator gun lines and 21/85 also aspirator another point all aspirators has 15th been investigated by a Gallium. One is collect division. Gang to carry at trans. from it it is naturally improvised with much chunkey before been hung aeroplane bombed one Bear Bde H.Q. at night - no damage. D.H.Orvin Lieut Or 9th Bde C.F.A.	

Confidential   *Original*

War Diary

of 9th Brigade Royal Field Artillery

From **1st** to **30th June 1918**.

Volume 6/1918.

HEADQUARTERS,
9TH BRIGADE,
R.F.A.
No. 1285
Date 2-4-18

Army Form C. 2118.

WAR DIARY
INTELLIGENCE SUMMARY.
(Erase heading not required.)

9th Brigade R.F.A. JUNE 1918

Place	Date	Hour	Summary of Events and Information	Remarks and references to Appendices
VIMY	1/6/18		Major R.M.A. Dunn 19th Bty rejoins from hospital. Enemy activity low except for some fair shelling. SHe	
Sunday	2/6/18		Enemy fairly active. A Scrambler 9 fires short chips from 4.2" Hows on to our artillery areas between 2am & 3am. 8" Howitzers shelled Dugouts & Heavy battery close to 9 A.B. Hqs from about 9am to 10am. No Casualties inconvenience but no damage. RE attend to Bty for lock purposes. Quiet night. SHe	
	3/6/18		28th Bty's two Klave buns withdrawn from its temporary position last night. Its ostin Koms cancelled at last moment. Wagon lines have also Known been moved but this was also cancelled. SHe	
	4/6/18		Wagon lines, everything 28th Bty's removed from LE PENDU & fired E. of ST ELOY. 35 Bty ordered to reconnoitre for wagon lines in vicinity of AUX RIETZ. 28 Bty moved spare Action B, 045 colone. Quiet night. Capt Longman, 19th Bty reported from leave. SHe	
	5/6/18		Congratulations from 9 Army Artillery on destructive shoot on a enemy Battery. Quiet night. SHe	
	6/6/18		18th Army Corps Commander visits 19th Bty. He takes a thorough inspection of S.O.S area trenches and the tasks of Harrassing means for 28 Bty. 28 Bty eight shoots on hostile Movement AA. Enemy made 2 heavy bombardment of area pnt N.9.9.4.5.4. Vimy from 9.15 & K about 10.15 am. A burst heard fired	

WAR DIARY
or
INTELLIGENCE SUMMARY.
(Erase heading not required.)

Army Form C. 2118.

Place	Date	Hour	Summary of Events and Information	Remarks and references to Appendices
VIMY	7/6/18		At least 300 shell. Read gas spot except for occasional shell on approaches of reinvisited front line defence, for batteries & HQs & approaches of reserve and lines of defence (Brown & Green lines). Night front except for some shelling of FAR SUD and SDN both took a second hundred hits & general calm on FAR SUD.	
	8/6/18		Aerial activity – Major ASHAM to 735 proceeded on leave. BGRA held conference with all Brigade Commanders as below re 901 new ground positions. In evening BGRA visits Brown line position. Relieved of Thin brigade and made a few alterations. Sgt Major HODGE to 20735 reported from leave.	
	9/6/18		Enemy carried out a destructive shoot on 6.2" howitzer 300± from 8/69 Htrs – very little damage & no casualties. At Commds. visited Brown line position. C.R.B.G Comdr to point out unk 76 Div. Quiet night. 20735 received a gun into (?workshop)	
	10/6/18		B.C.R.A. 52nd Div visited forward Hdrs. 5/69 Bty at 10.30am. 20735 registered forward gun. Forward guns 5/69, 19- + 20 - carried out harassing fire during night. Quiet night. Bde Commdr visited troops lines, 28 DB5 moved troop lines from LE PENDU to near Cadwmoet. Fd. two guns of 28 of 5/69 carried out gas bombard for two flurries of 3 minutes & other harassing fire during night.	
BERTHONVAL FARM	11/6/18			

Army Form C. 2118.

WAR DIARY
or
INTELLIGENCE SUMMARY.
(Erase heading not required.)

J. R. B^{de} R.A.

Instructions regarding War Diaries and Intelligence Summaries are contained in F.S. Regs., Part II. and the Staff Manual respectively. Title pages will be prepared in manuscript.

Place	Date	Hour	Summary of Events and Information	Remarks and references to Appendices
VIMY	12/4/18	7.15	One officer from HQ & one officer per battery forward under orders promised to visit the division on our left with a view to reconnoitring Bm positions for occupation in case the artillery of that division requiring reinforcement. Quiet night. Several explosions occurring from a type of trench mortar (probably) due to hung ammunition. This information forwarded to Corps. Carried on harassing fire during night - 60 rounds per gun. [sig]	
	13/4/18		Enemy carried out a destructive shoot with 4.2" Hows on 19"BY forward gun. No casualties. Damage but it is necessary to shift the gun. Work on Berm his position progressing very slowly as Works Bn Coys. Employed have sent men of low medical category. Camouflage for alternative position is very scarce & work is impeded by its absence. Usual harassing fire at night. Subsequent orders for barrage & Counter Battery position vicinity of ARLEUX received & issued. [sig]	
	14/4/18		19"BY moved forward gun about 200 yds. A.T.V. Selected sites for alternative O.P.s. BOCA examined OP. Coincided positions and is explained future policy. The reasonable slight rearrangement of batteries in Berm his position & QRA Coys full back to their position in line & being in line as at present. Forward from Coys as in organisation on the front of the division on our right. [sig]	
	15/4/18		Selected two new positions for 13/BY & 28/BY & reports sent in for approval. These positions even Berm line & new prepared line of resistance. SP. RA. XVIII Corps intimated his intention of inspecting 20"BY & 19/BY tomorrow at 11.15 am, [sig]	

WAR DIARY

INTELLIGENCE SUMMARY

9th Brigade R.F.A.

Army Form C. 2118.

Place	Date	Hour	Summary of Events and Information	Remarks and references to Appendices
VIMY	16/6/18		B.G.R.A. 52nd Div. visited BROWN Line positions and approved of new sites for 28th Bty/69 Battalion. G.O.C. R.A. XVIII Corps inspected 20th Bty at 11:15am in stable orders & remarked on the goodness of the horses. Naturally the 56th Bty did not hand over their best horses.	
		5 a.m.	Enemy artillery more active than usual & several rounds fell near Brigade HQrs. Enemy	
		11 am	attempts a distinction shoot on a target about 500 x NE of 28th HQrs. Three enemy kite balloons up than usual. Quiet night. S/L/D	
	17/6/18		Aerial activity fairly than usual. Fire effect of hostile shoots on of [illegible]. Hostile Ammunition dumps... (illegible) return less than normal. S/L/D	
	18/6/18		Major A. BLACK D.S.O. 20th Bty R.F.A. admitted to hospital. G/C. XVIII Corps inspected 19th, 28th & B/69 Bty began line & saw three batteries at drill. Remarked on the goodness of the remounts of the 19th & 28th Btys. Most of which were received from the 56th Bty. The animals were received in a very poor condition & it is doubtful if they will ever become really good. Both artillery smaller than... S/L/D	
	19/6/18		Steady rain in morning. Quiet night. Orders received regarding number of rounds for 18 pdr O.S. not reduced to bty 2 for 1st line target & 12 + 8 extra allowed on spare. 1st line target still. One pr. has two of every 10th Bty. Carried out instructional shoots with two of their 19th Bty. Enemy artillery quiet. S/L/D	
	20/6/18		Quiet night. Saw B/69 19th & 20th Bty at firm line during morning and in afternoon two officers of each of these batteries in actual shooting during afternoon. Major BURKE D.S.O. rejoined 28th Bty	

(A6004) Wt.W17771/M2931 75,000 5/17 D.D. & L., London, E.C. Sch. 52 Forms C2118/14

WAR DIARY
INTELLIGENCE SUMMARY

9th Bty R.F.A.   June 1918

Place	Date	Hour	Summary of Events and Information	Remarks and references to Appendices
	21/6/18		2nd Lieut attached 57th Bde Staff. Lieut ALTREE M.C. 28/B/35 admitted hospital. Quiet night. A little rain in evening. Fine day.	
	22/6/18		Saw O.C. & 28/B/340 at gun drill during morning. Adjutant & 2 officers of Brigade presented knavrays for a demonstration of tanks. Dull day. Being very quiet.	
	22/6/18		Received orders. Staff and Group (Right) of 52nd Div. on 26th inst from OC 52-13th RGA. Lt evening called to Group HQ & discussed arrange for new aggression line. Brown his position at the handed over to 52 Bde RGA. 2/Lt J LYDDAN joined 20/B/35 on promotion from B/108/13th RGA.	
Sunday	23/6/18		Enemy very quiet all night & 22/23. B.S.RA 52 Div. in reserve some 17 Riding horses arrived & transported from 9th KGDhSrRGA. Approved gas. except two. Bt. Car ordered to relieve the personnel. On return found that B/69/B5 had been ordered to move to position of the guns form for a special question. Move (the place at night and chemical shell 25.2D M/m from 8th GA up. Ammunition fails to come up correctly. The place and 7 up HE misses yesterday. Battery never been & got into action.	
	24/6/18		Quiet night but at 7.05 am enemy started bombardment for a short on heavy VS. position 570 + E. 9 G. & SH. HP. Ammunition for B/69 came up in sufficient & was run forward to light railway under cover & rain storm. At 9.30am B/69 & forward gun 28/B/35 took part in counter attack with chemical shell of enemy trenches near MERICOURT firing 55 do Chem.	

Army Form C. 2118.

WAR DIARY
INTELLIGENCE SUMMARY.
(Erase heading not required.)

9/2 B 52 RFA   June 918.

Place	Date	Hour	Summary of Events and Information	Remarks and references to Appendices
VIMY 25/6/18	25/6/18		ical fire hour to 80 rds HE for ground gun. After the bombardment B/by with other B'ies main position leaving two how: forward. 2/Lt STANLEY, who's gun proved on leave. Quiet night. JHE	
	26/6/18		Major N. ASHAM rejoined 19.35 from leave. B'by B Sgm Gun was affected severely by premier epidemic (influenza (debacles 5 Th melted as P.V.O. no apparel it is an obscure disease) the morale got a bit low has been glad in the brigade but the rest of the operation time… representative to be through his by it + certain units of the division has suffered heavily. JHE	
	26/6/18		B/H Hg took over command of the Right Group 52 D S. from Mr. ST Many 20th RFA who had done a good turn in West Battries at present forming the group on. 9/25E (19 20 23 mpgs) 17/36 and 951. Batteries 9th & B'ies between on the alternate provision of forum and position by between 9th. 52 D.S. Later act as subgroup to right group J/Hg	
	27/6/18		Orders received that infantry were take up new defensive line from from 3 ought where had the arranged accordingly. Through enemy outposts a new apparent outposts two really opposed by a weak militarised line and then the nuisance defence a distance of about a mile from the enemy front line could be made good by a weak french outlet barrage. JHE	
	28/6/18		CRA 52 D. inspected new provision being done by Bigour for the forum line. Quiet 7pm enemy opened fire with 77 men SE from HBs firing about 60 rounds, 20 shells a day of prey HBs firing about 60 rounds, 20 shells	

WAR DIARY
INTELLIGENCE SUMMARY.

9/13 ARTY June 1918

Place	Date	Hour	Summary of Events and Information	Remarks and references to Appendices
	29/6/18		G/112 Bty relieved A/152 Bty & A/112 relieved C/152 Bty in position with 9/13th Corps at 9.30pm. Quiet night. JWE	
			CRA called conference of Bde Commanders at dept from HQrs. Discussed training of Battalions & open warfare tactical shooting & ordered Bde CO's to reconnoitre & see if there are any places on the Div. front where guns could be shoved into positions to fire openly on the enemy. Issued orders that from Tomorrow on 3 guns were to be kept forward and one moving gun, also 1 how. forward. At night forward gun Tressed harassing fire onto suspected relief of German division from Hugo Group 2203.25. 18P9 & 2120.25. 4-5" JWE	
Sunday	30/6/18		Enemy shelled forward gun area but did no damage. Large lines also received attention from a H.V. gun. Bourle.	

HJCarter
Lt Col RA
Commg 9 Brigade RFA

Increases and Decreases in personnel for month of June 1918.

Increase.

Officers.	Other Ranks.		Remarks.
	From Hospital	Reinforcements.	
2.*	10.	25.	*: Major T.M. Adam, rejoined from Hospital. Lieut. J. Lyddon. Joined from B/106. Brigade R.F.A.

Decrease.

Officers.	Other Ranks.		Remarks.
	To Hospital	Commissioned.	
1.⊗	40.	2.#	⊗ Major A. Black. N.3.O. to Hospital (sick). # 63654. Corpl. A.E. Cockaday. Appointed Lieut. 12-6-18. 47224. B.Q.M.S. W. Ernest. " " 12-6-18.

Winter
Lieut.-Col. R.A.
Commanding 9th Brigade R.F.A.

Confidential.   *Original.*

Vol 4

War Diary
of
9th Brigade Royal Field Artillery.

From 1st to 31st July 1918.

Volume 7/1918.

HEADQUARTERS,
9TH BRIGADE,
R.F.A.
No. 1751
Date 1-8-18.

Army Form C. 2118.

WAR DIARY
INTELLIGENCE SUMMARY.
(Erase heading not required.)

9th Brigade R.F.A.   July 1918

Place	Date	Hour	Summary of Events and Information	Remarks and references to Appendices
VIMY	1/7/18		Forward gun area heavily shelled by 77 mm. No damage or casualties. Enemy MG wire quiet.	
	2/7/18		Lt Mayers 78th/RFA proceed on leave. Capt Allbury proceed from leave. J. Boyd transferred to 52nd RFA (S.S.). Enemy compensating shoot ff S 8.b.0.0 & H.18.a.0.0.5 - 14 RFA according to HDDM. Forward gun area again heavily shelled from 7.30 to 9 am & 11.77mm.	
	3/7/18			
	4/7/18		Quiet night. B.G.R.A visits group & inspects proposed Battle Station for forward guns. Lt Upson 81st/RFA hospital. Capt Allbury reports for duty with 20 R.F.A. vice Capt J. Boyd transferred to 52nd RFA.	
	5/7/18		Capt Allbury's Jimmy postponed. Capt N.C.W Pringle from 122 RFA. posted & command 20 R.F.A. temp. of Brigadier visits wagon lines and inspects the alterations upon his side. Enemy opened fire with H.V. gun on Brigade HQ - no casualties.	
	6/7/18		Brig N.C.W Pringle joined 20 R.F.A. N°8.60.40 & A.T. Boggust Reg. VS. officer in Field Ambulance. Col rejoined from leave.	
Sunday	7/7/18		B.G.R.A inspects Brown line positions. B.H. Cdrs held conference of Bty Commanders. Enemy put a few shells on our rear gunners Bde sheet 44.2.	
	8/7/18		B.C.R.A. visits Battery positions of 9 & 93 Cdr during morning. Batteries of 9.R. Bde detailed to take part in minor operation of 152nd RFA. (51st Div) on our right.	

WAR DIARY

INTELLIGENCE SUMMARY

9 Bde RFA   (Erase heading not required.)   **July 1918**

Army Form C. 2118.

Place	Date	Hour	Summary of Events and Information	Remarks and references to Appendices
VIMY	9/7/18		19, 20, 28 & D/69 batteries supported minor operation of 51/25 (XVII Corps) on our right. Raid into AREUX Loop & reserve line trenches. Zero hour was 12.30am, and bombardment lasted 40 mins of which first 5 were intense. At 11. own enemy aeroplane brought down in flames just E of FARBUS by one of our escorts. Selected main battle stations for two forward groups. Ack. Maj J HICKEY from	
	10/7/18		Very quiet night. Nothing to note. Relief Maj J HICKEY left for attachment to Staff VIII Corps.	
	11/7/18		Quiet day. Lieut R J MORFEY rejoined Brigade & posted to 20/734. Sgt BEER returned from signalling course.	
	12/7/18		A few gas shells were shot after midnight - no ill effects. 52/43rd (Army) FA ordered to be relieved from Right Group by 8th Canadian FA Bde.	
	13/7/18		Gas Alarm propelled at 12.30am Ordr MERCURY Code. Forward guns carried out harassing fire from 1.30am to 6.30am on area that had been gassed. 2/Lt UPSON rejoined 5/69 from hospital. D/69 BS carried out shoot with air burst ranging. First time battery & Field Survey Co. had done it in procedure in close but apparent accurate.	
Sunday	14/7/18		Forward guns carried out harassing fire on same area as last night - double naval allotment too fired heavy Trench Mortar. Capt V LONGMAN joined HQ Kitchener to 2/Lieut V. WALSHE proceeding on leave. At 10pm received orders the group would be reorganised.	

Army Form C. 2118.

WAR DIARY

INTELLIGENCE SUMMARY

9th Bde RFA   July 1918.

(Erase heading not required.)

Instructions regarding War Diaries and Intelligence Summaries are contained in F. S. Regs., Part II. and the Staff Manual respectively. Title pages will be prepared in manuscript.

Place	Date	Hour	Summary of Events and Information	Remarks and references to Appendices
VIMY	15/7/18		At 3 am received intimation that 512th B had been relieved by 8" Canadian F.A. Letter received instr Rep Group FUs 9 am 16th. After Adv Group wire cones of 9th Bde RFA + 242nd Army Bde RFA of little 2 batteries (A/15) who proved to be read for training together with HQ of 242nd D.A.H. These batteries go out on night of 16/7/17. Wired Composite Battery Commanders in evening to discuss new bumps & new infantry dispositions. Capt AM SMYTHE. M.C. 25th B/S rejoined from leave F.U.K. 20th B/S moved bump line & FORT GEORGE about 1/2 mile nearer frm line. JHC	Bomar's communication in operations in ARGONNE received etc in GHQ communique
	16/7/18		Heavy thunderstorm at 3am. Daytime hotter. Major S.F. BURNE DSO proceed on leave F.U.K. JHC	
	17/7/18		Weather much warmer. 20th B/S were bombed by aeroplane abt 1-2 30 am, no damage & personnel & no signal damage to a truck. JHC	
	18/7/18		25th B/S inf adv on sector began. Divn to start under Scottish Division after 3rd B. MGRA 1st Army - Maj Gen E.W. ALEXANDER CMG DSO visited Group. JHC	
	19/7/18		OC Brigade and representatives of various Brigades reconnoitred GHQ Line. On return met Brigadier who brought news that Brigade would be retired in the line in the course of the next few days to 5, 8 = 19th A + moved forward to XVII Corps area to join 16th Corps. OC to also moved to 16., 20th + 25th Bdys to create present positions, which are refused (Canadian Corps and move to alternative positions N.g. THELUS. These posn were committed on fair linen later. JHC	

Army Form C. 2118.

WAR DIARY
INTELLIGENCE SUMMARY.

(Erase heading not required.)

9 Bde RFA   July 1918.

Place	Date	Hour	Summary of Events and Information	Remarks and references to Appendices
TINY	20/7/18		Enemy put about 50 shell near group H.Q. At 10 am 33rd Bde RFA arrived & took over group. Advance parties took over wagon lines by LA TARGETTE. A section guns & batteries retired a section of batteries of 9th Bde RFA during night 20/21. A/C	
	21/7/18		Enemy shelled vicinity of group HQ with 77 mm & 4.2 cm. Some gas shell mixed up with these shelling Nr CAUCOURT. 19th & 20th Bdes also report similar gas report about 20 shell – phosgene. At 10 pm Lt Col D.E. FORMAN Comdr & officers 33rd Bde R. FA arrived to finally take over group. Command passed at 8 pm. After dark, remaining sections of batteries withdrew on relief by 33rd Bde and went to the wagon lines. Left stores & effects vid'd General. A/C	
HERSIN	22/7/18		Batteries reported by 1 am that they were in wagon lines. Corps are passing through. At 9.0 am brigade marched to billets in XVII Corps area passing starting point near Mt St ELOY to following order 19th Bde, 9.10 am; 2/59, 9.25 am; HQ & 58th at 9.40; & D/255 at 9.55 am; 19th Bde billets at BARAFFLE, B/59, 28th A/42 at HERMIN and 30 Bty at GAUCHIN-LEGAL. Billets scarce & no mess of the men were in tents of billets Hein was a scarcity. Camps crowded - chilly. A/C	
	23/7/18		Heavy rain most of the morning. Antipasta received in evening move billets to 19th & 20th Bdes. Capt. J. BOYD left the 20th Bty from 52nd DAC, and was replaced by Capt. ALBAN from 52nd DAC. 2nd Lt from 30 Bde on leave from 7 day. A/C	
	24/7/18		Batteries HQ overseeing moved to ACQ & CALONNE - RICOUART (19th Bde) 60 Brigade entrained at their points in evening & moved by rail. HQ & 23 Bty at ACQ & 19th Bde at CALONNE. A/C	

Army Form C. 2118.

WAR DIARY

INTELLIGENCE SUMMARY.

(Erase heading not required.)

9 Bde. R.F.A.   July 1918

Instructions regarding War Diaries and Intelligence Summaries are contained in F. S. Regs., Part II. and the Staff Manual respectively. Title pages will be prepared in manuscript.

Place	Date	Hour	Summary of Events and Information	Remarks and references to Appendices
HERMIN. Pas de Calais	25/7/18		Attended Conference at 52nd DA HQ respecting a staff scheme. Horse & limber of the 29 & 30 mortar firing RLA Conference 9 Bde. in connection with they exercise. SMC	
	26/7/18		Bde Comdg. attended Conference held by G.O.C RA XVII Corps in connection with Coing exercise. Conference held at AUBIGNY. Capt A.W. SMITHE A/C promoted Lieutenant in Battery Commander Course working at WESTCLIFFE on 28 July. SMC	
	27/7/18		Last morning. Lt de KOTE Bega RS reported from leave. RTK relieves Wren temporary Command 9/28th 134y. SMC	
	28/7/18		OC Brigade went with OC 57 154, 9/39 RD 52 D. to 6 Div HQ at ABEELE in YPRES salient to see position which it is contemplated will be occupied hereafter. This circumstance of Battries 9/53: 57. Returned same evening & fixed orders Concerning Staff tactics & hand centrally that 52 DA would move tomorrow & supply lines of MADAGASCAR Camp preparator to relieving 5 Canadian DA in Salient N of ARRAS. SMC	
MADAGASCAR Camp	29/7/18		Orders received at 5 am to march to MADAGASCAR Camp. 9 Bde. RFA the clear of Cross roads at SAUCHIN-LE-Comt by 9 am & in camp by 2 pm. OC WAS picked to see OC 13° Coy RH Arters in the brigade Kth relieved by us. Units were	

WAR DIARY
INTELLIGENCE SUMMARY.

9th Bde R.F.A.   July, 1918.

Place	Date	Hour	Summary of Events and Information	Remarks and references to Appendices
North of R.SCARPE NE of ARRAS HQ at H.7.a.1.2.	30/7/18		In camp by 4 pm. Transport was very short as a large amount of extra ammn had been accumulated & had to be carried. Transport for batts went into position at night.	
			Settling down by batteries. Most dug in. Completed by 10.30 pm. Battalion relieving on flanks. 15th - 52nd CFB, 30th - 53rd, 25th - 55th and 57th - 57th Nov 55. The batty positions & living places are excellent & much use has been put in them. Dugouts in many lines (where the front system & within them can a change of front was possible) is made. The OPs are not too good, having few distinct battery areas – chiefly tea & map but to concentrate was not very satisfactory.	
	31/7/18		Normal activity during day. 18 Pdr Bty moved a gun each in to the position to upset gaps during tomorrow (firing the enemy the impression that no batteries had come in & were registering). Late at night received partial in formation that Bde would be to move bombarded during early hours of morning. HQ, 20th & 21st, 30th Bde moved hostile. Reinforcements with ejected from their positions as they are in another divisional area. 4th Canadian D.A. orders received giving new barrage lines – 9 & 58 Bde RFA and superimposed on barrages of 56 & 58 Bde RFA & part of 3rd Cdn DA – a front of 2500ˣ.	

A.N. Davies
Lt Col
Comdg 9th Bde RFA

Increase & Decrease in personnel for month of July 1918

Increase.

Officers	Other Ranks		Remarks
	From Hospital	Reinforcements	
4.	54.	49.	Major W.C. Watt Pringle. Joined from 122 By. R.F.A. 6-7-18 Lieut: P.J. Mosley. Rejoined from leave to U.K. 11-7-18 Lieut: D.M. Upson. Rejoined from Hospital 12-7-18. Capt: Z.C.H. Alban. Joined from 52nd D.A.C. 23-7-18.

Decrease.

Officers	Other Ranks		Remarks
	To Hospital	Commissioned	
1.	59.	2.	Capt: J. Boyd. Posted to 52nd D.A.C. 23-7-18. 7⁰⁶1963 Sergt: Coase. S.H. Appointed Lieutenant 7-7-18. 7⁰⁵5735 Sergt: Ralph. H.B. " 15-7-18.

F.R. Ongman. Capt. R.F.A.
for —
Lieut Col. R.A.
Commanding J. Brigade R.F.A.

Confidential *Original*

Vol 5

War Diary
of
9th Brigade Royal Field Artillery
from
1st Aug to 31st August 1918.

Volume 8/1918.

HEADQUARTERS,
9TH BRIGADE,
R.F.A.
No. 163.
Date.

WAR DIARY
INTELLIGENCE SUMMARY.

9th Brigade R.F.A. August 1918.

Place	Date	Hour	Summary of Events and Information	Remarks and references to Appendices
NE of RRAS H7.a.1.2.	1/8/18	2 am	9/BDE RFA main t/found gun carried out 10 minutes bombardment of August to N. GAVRELLE. Enemy shelled 28th B.S. position during morning at intervals and his one gun pit damaging the crew. No casualties. Enemy 5.9 howitzer number of gas shells came over at various times but caused no inconvenience. BGRA 52nd Dt. visited B.S. position & returned 20.25 & 31st position. B.S. 14th Bde orders to look for new place as present locatn. is in 57th Dt. area. two prisoners taken. G87/69 area saw sundry air alarms. Apparent. 20°85 moved after dark into new position. P.C. 13.12.39 Lieut KNIGHT 28th BS. wounded about 9.30pm Transmitted hospital	S/18
	2/8/18		OC Brigade accom. to D.A. H.Q. STAKE on tour temp. duties as GRA & Col. MUSGRAVE slightly wounded. Major ADAM assumed temporary command of the Brigade. W. POWELL proceeded on leave. A quiet day owing to mist and rain. Usual N.H.F. at night.	S/18
	3/8/18		Bde HQs moved to H.I.C.70.65 at midday. Battery S.O.S. tasks readjusted to suit move of Batteries. Major S.F. BURNE DSO rejoined from leave.	S/18
Sunday	4/8/18		Lieut COTTER resumed command on Brig.Gen. MUSGRAVE returning to command of 52nd D.A. Major J.P. HICKEY returned to command 37/69 Bty from Corse as learner at VIII Corps HQ. Lieut BECKER rejoined from Corse as learner at 1st Army School of Gunnery.	S/18
	5/8/18		Orders that Bde HQs would move to ROEINCOURT on 7/8/18. August received. Section 19 & 37/69 wire section (y/A/277-D/77) in position occupied by latter battn. which now operates fwd. of N.E. Remaining section move in night 6/7. June 10 am 8/1 one of OC g.BS. will function as OC Centre front consisting 157th Army Bde. Dep B.Bde. Group will consist of 19, 20, 37/69 and B + C +D/277 R.A.	S/18

Army Form C. 2118.

WAR DIARY
INTELLIGENCE SUMMARY.
(Erase heading not required.)

9th Brigade RFA August 1918

Instructions regarding War Diaries and Intelligence Summaries are contained in F. S. Regs., Part II. and the Staff Manual respectively. Title pages will be prepared in manuscript.

Place	Date	Hour	Summary of Events and Information	Remarks and references to Appendices
H.I.C.70.65. (MARQUEUIL)	6/8/18		Remainder of 19th Bde. & 51/54 B5 moved to new positions in Approach A 29 & A 30. Forward gun remains in front position temporarily. Lieut WOOLLACOTT on leave.	SF8
	7/8/18	2am	Brigade received night harassing fire in conjunction with the 3pdr. Co-operation of troops OPPY.	SF8
		2.45pm	Lieut E.O. PARROTT 19/B5 killed by chance shelling of Battn. position. Shells burst close on own 18pdr.	
			2 men 20/B4 slightly wounded during night and 1 Sergt., 2 Cpls 18pdr + 3 men 28/B5 gassed and sent to hospital during night. *20.105. Bmb. G. W. CLARKE P. 159321 from STORRIE W.	
			P.28 B5. 65145 Sgt TAYLOR C.S. Cpls 151 PHILLIPS A. 77773. LiS. SAPSFORD 902nd Cpl HENDERSON A. 70857, & YOUNGS R. 107312, Gnr FAWCETT G.C.	
		10 pm	HQ moved to ROCLINCOURT A.29 & 8.6. Being astronomical HQs of H.I.C.70.65.	
ROCLINCOURT	8/8/18	10.4am	Lt Col H.J. COTTER & 9th Bde. HQ staff took on command of Centre group 52nd RFA from Lt Col J. COCHRANE 50. RFA Commanding 272nd Army Bde RFA.	SF8
		3pm	Arrived Lt PARRITT at ROCLINCOURT. H.V. gun shelling ECURIE during night & continued with enemy shots from first hit about 4am. This gun particularly troublesome for air harassing fire and 5/10 Argyll... Rest. place about 12.30am (9th)	SF8
	9/8/18		2 Ln Davis 1 Cook from 52 D.A.C. temporarily loaned 19th Bde army Esplenails 9 Strand.	SF8
			Received 20/B5 9/8/18 11.15am a gunner from Base.	
	10/8/18		Visited Major LUNN - 19/B4 Quippis & new target Linen, being rather active in forward gun areas.	SF8
	11/8/18	3am	Enemy firing on our forward trenches.	SF8
		3.8am	S.O.S. signal went up & our response to at once. Rate of fire 4 rds per min., slowing up after 10 minutes. No information. Coasca la Marmia a.k. & the first the S.O.S. up. Approach on Centre group front reported all quiet about 3.30am.	

D.D. & L., London, E.C. (A5001) Wt. W1771/M2034. 750,000. 5/17. Sch. 52. Forms C/2118/14

WAR DIARY
INTELLIGENCE SUMMARY.

(Erase heading not required.) August 1918   J.H.Bryan R.R.A

Place	Date	Hour	Summary of Events and Information	Remarks and references to Appendices
RICOURT	12/8/18		Ceas fire was ordered at 3.50 am Relief occurs Than been opposite GRAVELLE which attack on left flank of division is on right thrown gun our position.	S/18
	13/8/18		OC Brigade ordered tactical lecture and demonstration by L.O. Francy (Gen MANSC) at Chateau LA HAYE - Quiet day. Enemy plans reported. Shar turned up a battalion for a short or 20.35. Nothing happened.	S/18
			Lieut Cotter proceeds to HQ 52"DM. Officials al CRA v. Brg.Gal MUSGRAVE DSO presents & baptized on Richmond. Mayor SELBURNE DSO takes over command of the group. Orders received in regard of 52" Div: by 51" Div: on night 14/15 and 15/16 August. Also for 277 Army Bde. to go out of action to rendez-vous night 14/15. Arty Orders always were to postponing owing few privately. LT BECKER on leave.	S/18
	14/8/18		Orders received for relief on dates as above, but by 45" Bde, 8" D.A. B/277 to left group, 28" Bty to "C" of the group.	S/18
	15/8/18		Handed over Lashe Group to 2/Col Brokwey DSC 45" Bde. R.F.A. Relief complete reported 3.45 am. Gun relieving bty. lost it's way, account for the delay.	S/18
	16/8/18 17/8/18		In Wagon line. Bombs dropped in vicinity about 1 pm Bde. marched to billets in ACQ about 4 pm. arriving 7 pm. Conference at RAHQ 62"Div of Bde. & D.A.C. Commanders. Orders to reconnoitre positions to support a local operation	S/18

WAR DIARY or INTELLIGENCE SUMMARY

August 1918   9th Bde. R.F.A.

Place	Date	Hour	Summary of Events and Information	Remarks and references to Appendices
ACQ	18.8.18		Positions reconnoitred E. of ARRAS. C.R.A. Bde Commander, B.C.'s & R.O.'s present. Digging parties (1 N.C.O. and 10 men) went up to prepare positions in the evening. Digging parties from billets about 9 pm. Orders received to be prepared to occupy positions night 19/20. Difficulty experienced in getting camouflage. 2/Lt Powell rejoined from leave. Orders received to stand fast, but to finish off the positions. Operations postponed.	S/AS
ACQ	19.8.18		Digging parties recalled. Bde Commander inspected positions, which were found to be very well dug & reflected great credit on the officers & men concerned. Orders to be ready to move tonight, subsequently cancelled, & orders given to be ready to move at short notice.	S/AS
ACQ	20.8.18		Marched & moved to BEAUMETZ-LES-LOGES, moving at 7.30 pm. Bright moonlight night. Enemy airoplane activity bombing – one E.A. seen to crash. S/AS	S/AS
BEAUMETZ	22.8.18		Arrived at destination about 1.15 am. 162851 pusion brother & father Casualties incurred Wounded 16585 2 Lt BEER.R, 148796 Cpl MACCULLUM A.D (since died) 23678 Dr MACPHERSON S.A, 52622 Dr WHEATLEY.F. Slight wounded & remaining at duty. 2- Lt KERRIDGE C.J 10587 Dr LINDFIELD G.L. Bde Commd. and Recce orders up to BLAIREVILLE & reconnoitr positions E of FICHEUX Bn occupies this night. Brigade moved into positions S/AS	S/AS

WAR DIARY / INTELLIGENCE SUMMARY

Army Form C. 2118.

Unit: 9/3 Bde R.F.A.
Month: August 1918 [May 1918]

Place	Date	Hour	Summary of Events and Information	Remarks and references to Appendices
Near FICHEUX	23/5/18		Brigade supported attack of 52 Div. Zero hour was at 4:58 am. First objectives captured.	
	24/5/18		Enemy took the road of Tanks and enemy counter-attacked. Lt. Col. H.J. COTTER rejoined & assumed command of Group. Casualties: 112577 Gnr. WHITLEY, 30134 Gnr. HASWELL, 2nd Bty. 96344 Gnr. TAYLOR. A/58 Bde. Enemy barrage at 6:55 am. 156 Brigade which was supplies by 5" Bde RFA & D/258 Bde RFA advanced their line. Brigade moved forward to cover support. Q58 Bde came under fire getting to their position. Suffered casualties: 30757 Bdr. KENDRICK B. 29th Bty. A/15/H.R.A. Gnr. GADD W. 4th Bty ROBERTS F. Kennedy? 29th Bty BDR. H.L.A.R? GREENFIELD? Q57 Sgt. [illegible], Q15057 Gnr. [illegible] from Stokes, 3 [illegible], from JAMES T. 77th [illegible] wounded. L/cpl U.G. GARTHER B. 43217 Cpl. WEBBER 14th Bty.	
Near MERCATEL	25/5/18		Harassed enemy at night & during day. Considerable advance secured by Bde Gp on road to HENIN. Quiet day as 52 Div action at same place.	
	26/5/18		Major BURNE reconnoitred forward for new position for Brigade. Orders received to move forward by night, but greatly counter-ordered when 28" Bty. had started. On its return it was shelled and we suffered casualties as below. In the afternoon a barrage was fired to cover infantry advance on HINDENBURG LINE.	
	27/5/18		Casualties: 114850 Gnr. SYMONS H.Q., 14th Bty. wounded, [illegible] Sgt. MILLERSON W.F.J and 114134 Bomb. HALL R. died of wounds, 28 Bty. 149168 Gnr. MCCORMICK W. [illegible], 66m STONE W. 5127 Dv JAMES T. 196 A/Gm GAMM J.H. 106012 Dv TURNER D. 29 Bty. wounded. Moved forward to position west of HENIN. Fired barrage at 10 am to cover attack by 157 Bde. on HINDE FONTAINE. Attack completely successful, many prisoners taken. H.Q. an area west of HENIN. 157 Inf. Bde. H.Q. in HINDENBURG LINE.	

WAR DIARY
or
INTELLIGENCE SUMMARY.

Army Form C. 2118.

Place	Date	Hour	Summary of Events and Information	Remarks and references to Appendices
	28/8/18		28th Stood uneventful 1 section to HINDENBURG LINE. 19th & 20th moved up late in afternoon & 28th Bty. completed move by night. 57th Div" Gen. D.A. relieved by 57th div" Gen. D.A. during night. J.C.H. Otter returned to his duties on C.R.A. S & D.A. Major S.F. Burne took command of Bde. Barrage fired from 12.30 to 2 in support of attack by 172 Bde. on HOOP LANE attack successful. 19th Bty. advanced into the open & were heavily shelled. Major M.M. Adam R.F.A. killed in action, & survivors less both to his battery & the Bde. (Casualties 28/8/18, 6mrs D.O.R.R.A.N. 19th Bty wounded).	S/13
	29/8/18		Advanced to positions near Fontaine. Brigade & Batteries to come under heavy still fire during the advance down an open forward slope under direct enemy observation. Horse casualties very serious. Barrage orders received 12.35 p.m. ZERO 1 p.m. batteries opened fire by 1.15 p.m. Attack successful, but enemy resistance hardening considerably. Fire very heavy during day & increasing at night. with much gas. Bde. S left with Aunch gas. B.K. WALKER R. No Bde S left <unclear> enemy <unclear> shared moved H.Q. at night to higher ground to	S/13

WAR DIARY
INTELLIGENCE SUMMARY

Army Form C. 2118.

Place	Date	Hour	Summary of Events and Information	Remarks and references to Appendices
	30/8/18		Avril. Sas shelters. Drawn 29.8 - 30.8 Casualties 701114 Bomr WALKER W. 707114 Gnr. LEISHMAN A.A. Details Offrs Capt. BATTS M. BLAND D. R. RUMNEY S.C. LIEUT. DAVIES B.A. and 14 & Bn. wounded. 535 S.S. Gnrs at DUTY Sergt. 2 & 6 Bn. wounded. 11 & 8 Bn. gassed. Cavendish and 67 O.R. Kept advanced ampler very sharp + a harassing fire in interval. Objective. Enemy counter attack on our front drove us out of RIENCOURT & HENDECOURT & div. on our right knocked back from BULLECOURT. S.O.S. Arrangements partially failed owing to difficulties in communication. Line was being constantly broken by enemy shell fire. Visual from F.O.Os impossible owing to conformation of ground. Bde H.Q. heavily shelled out again with 5.9 & 4.2 how. all day, especially heavy at 2 p.m. Moved H.Q. at night to less exposed position. The forward H.Q. being under direct observation. During 29./8./30 th the morning of 30th. Signals by LT. MADGWICK was beyond all praise. The lines were constantly being repaired under heavy shell fire & SERGT. McRAE & the linesmen did extremely good work. The gunners were commended for immediate arrival of casualties were heavily shelled all day with the exception of D/69 Batteries. CARR. W. 315257 Gnr. HILL P. T. with 2 & 6 Bn. wounded. 42895 Gnr. CARR. W. 315259 Gnr. HILL P. T. with 2 & 6 Bn. wounded.	S.A.

WAR DIARY
or
INTELLIGENCE SUMMARY.

Army Form C. 2118.

Place	Date	Hour	Summary of Events and Information	Remarks and references to Appendices
FONTAINE-LEZ CROISILLES	31/8/18		No move. Quiet day. Batteries were shelled intermittently. Orders received for a barrage next morning, to cover infantry attack on HENDECOURT. Casualties Sgt. Stanton .T. wounded 20th Bty	attack on HENDECOURT
	1/9/18		Same place. Barrage opened at 4.50 a.m. Infantry attack successful. Capt. V.S. Longman killed. Had very good loss. Orders received for barrage to cover break through on ECOURT - QUEANT line.	
	2/9/18			

S.S Sumner Major R.A.
Cmdg 91st Bde R.F.A.

Confidential. Original.

52 Divn

War Diary

of 9th Brigade Royal Field Artillery.

from

1st to 30th September 1918.

Volume 9/1918.

WAR DIARY or INTELLIGENCE SUMMARY

Army Form C. 2118.

9th Brigade R.F.A.   September 1918.

Place	Date	Hour	Summary of Events and Information	Remarks and references to Appendices
FONTAINE-LEZ-CROISILLES	1-9-18		Barrage fired 4:50 a.m. Advance completely successful, and objectives killed. 2Lieut. W.S. Long was killed in action. Of great era. Orders for his attack to break DROCOURT-QUEANT Line. Casualties killed 265807 Gnr. Corpl. A.J. 28th Bty, Wounded 107166 S/S. Harkness W.A. Bty. II; Bm. Vines, 2nd Lieut. J. Kelridge No. 11th Bty, 44525 Gnr. Bracken E. 28th Bty, 1318 RB. Gnr. Philipson, 280 Gun Charmer N.W. 312397 Gnr. Yuhnsey P. (Field Amb. writing with mother) Barrage fired at 5 a.m. This a creeping barrage to confirm to Canadian barrage on left, then a switching barrage to allow our infantry to go through gap made by Canadians & wheel to the right down DROCOURT line. Operation very successful. Adv. to HENDECOURT. Men to about 2 kilo N. of CASSILCOURT. Infantry went forward rapidly with little opposition. Owing to confusion of infantry below advance took some time. Very little firing after barrage finished. Casualties about 6 in. 9th Bde. F. Hounsell, 2nd Bty.	
CAGNICOURT	2-9-18			
PRONVILLE	3-9-18		Same position. Brigade advanced during morning to positions about 1 kilom. S.S.W. of BOIS DE BOUCHE. Further advance in evening to positions about 1½ kilom. N.E. of PRONVILLE. During day in posy. worked through INCHY. Casualties killed 37/310 Dvr. Leighton F.G., Wrs. N.E. Sub. Section, wounded 1113300 Gnr. Worrall W.H., 28th Bty.	
	4-9-18		Same position. Infantry advancing to gain line of CANAL DU NORD. Reconnoitred new positions about 1 kilom. S. of INCHY. Saw enemy counter attacked about 7.0 p.m. Batteries fired S.O.S. & barrage on CANAL DU NORD. Stew enemy got in to N.E. corner of INCHY. Ordinary H.F. at night. Casualties wounded 302884 Dvr. OCRNSTEYN(?)	

Confidential.   Original.

52 Divn

War Diary

of

9th Brigade Royal Field Artillery.

from

1st to 30th September 1918.

Volume 9/1918.

WAR DIARY or INTELLIGENCE SUMMARY

9th Brigade R.F.A. September 1918

Place	Date	Hour	Summary of Events and Information	Remarks and references to Appendices
FONTAINE-LEZ-CROISILLES	1.9.18		Barrage fired 4.50 a.m. Advance completely successful, and objectives held. 2/Lieut. W.S. Long man killed in action. 3 gas cas. Orders for his attack to break DROCOURT-QUEANT Line. Casualties killed 26580 Gnr. Al Little Bay, Wounded 105113 Sgt. Hankes W.P. Gnr. H. Brunsey, 2nd Lieut. Kendrick W.H., 144581 Gnr. Anstie, 144354 Gnr. Bracketeye, 2914 Gnr. 132 Pl. Gnr. Philipson, 2830 Gnr. Chapman W.W. 26427 Gnr. Unsey, 180340 Gnr. Whiting W.G., all off B.	
CAGNICOURT	2.9.18	5 a.m.	Barrage fired at 5 a.m. Two o'clock, barrage to conform to Canadian barrage on left. The a switching barrage to allow our infantry to go through gap made by Canadians while the night down DROCOURT line. Operation very successful. Advanced to HENDECOURT then to about 2 kilos W. of CASS-COURT. Infantry went forward rapidly with little opposition. Owing to confusion of infantry advance not done. Few very little firing after barrage finished. Casualties wounded Bom. Stannard.F. Wounded, Bty.	
PRONVILLE	3.9.18		Same position. Brigade advanced during morning to positions about 1 kilom. S.S.W. of BOIS DE BOUCHE. Further advance in evening to positions about 1½ kilom. N.E. B/W of PRONVILLE. Quiet day in early works through INCHY. Casualties killed 311310 Bmr. LEIGHTON F.G. Kilpro R.E. sub drawn, Wounded 1113411 Gnr. Worrall W.H. Hutchinson 18th Bty.	
	4.9.18		Same position. Infantry advancing to gain line of CANAL DU NORD. Reconnoitred new positions about 1 kilom. S. of INCHY. Saw enemy counter attacked about 7 p.m. Batteries fired S.O.S. & barrage on CANAL DU NORD. A few enemy got into N.E. corner of INCHY. Ordinary H.F. at night by Searchlight Howitzer 289 Bty. 18 ton 2nd Bty.	

Army Form C. 2118.

WAR DIARY
or
INTELLIGENCE SUMMARY.
(Erase heading not required.)

Sept 1918   9th Bde RFA

Instructions regarding War Diaries and Intelligence Summaries are contained in F. S. Regs., Part II. and the Staff Manual respectively. Title pages will be prepared in manuscript.

Place	Date	Hour	Summary of Events and Information	Remarks and references to Appendices
Sept	5.9.18		Harassing fire and registration. H.Q. shelled, 3 O.R. casualties. Otherwise quiet day. N° Gunner ARMSTRONG, N° Gunner BAKER 28th/25 acting as orderlies at Bde HQ, the killed and N° Gunner BERTON, 9th/25 lightly wounded. JH/c	
near PRONVILLE	6.9.18		Brigade carried out usual harassing fire. Enemy shelling intermittent & lighter. 70 recruits trades received and 27 O.R. reinforcements. JH/c	
	7.9.18	5.30 p	A counter barrage fire was ordered if 63rd RN Div. to which Brigade is now attached. This barrage reached S. slopes of BOURLON WOOD hill. Sources wasteful of ammunition & little result apparent. Only 1 or 2 enemy of the greatest for day's enemy moved to barrage has been practiced hit. Ordered to keep 300 rds. per 18 pdr. & 250 rds 4.5" at guns. JH/c	
	8.9.18		57th Div relieved 63rd RN Div. 9th Brigade ordered to become & remain brigade from 6 pm onwards, the liaison officer having been taken over by 285th B de RFA. 9.13 & I.Z. ordered by X pie on S.O.S. call. Storage battery orders I got up 300 rds 18m shell. Began live. oblig 65 truck 4 new BULLECOURT. On return of 181 for MUSGROVE DSO from hospital Lt Col H.J CUTTER resumed command of Brigade. Heavy rain storm in afternoon. Comparatively quiet day. JH/c	
	9/9/18		Capt. A.W. SMYTHE. M.C. on rejoining from course at SALISBURY assumed command of 19 Bty. a Major D. BIRD. A/C. 5tm vgt. 5B/Bde RFA. Quiet day. Enemy artillery will with enter your trenches. JH/c	

WAR DIARY

INTELLIGENCE SUMMARY

G "B" R.F.A. — Sept 1918

Army Form C. 2118.

Place	Date	Hour	Summary of Events and Information	Remarks and references to Appendices
PRONVILLE	10/9/18		Last night enemy gas shells were but very slight and caused no inconvenience. Quiet day. JHL	4 Bars Sgt A.M.19.109 E-52 cl. caps
	11/9/18	11:30am	O.C. Comdr. attended conference at 57th D.I.A. H.Q. and received orders as barrage at 6.15pm under which, in cooperation with corps on our right, an attack was to be made to secure line of CANAL DU-NORD. This battery – 16 guns – allotted an area east of MOEUVRES & 184 yds in breadth to harass area – 28 yds. (enemy) as our E.P.MCHY. At 4.30 pm SOS call from Right Brigade. Answered + firing stopped on supp. Apparently false alarm. Clue to enemy putting up a barrage. At 6.15pm Company barrage fired + advance made. Enemy put on right but apparently unsuccessful in counter as SOS line was brought back several times + later on to 200° W. of CANAL. JHL	73/88 Sgt STANTON 30/4/85 87/88 R WELCHI 26/85 as an C.O. Military merit
	12/9/18		At about 3.45 am heavy barrage on our right + heavy artillery barrage commenced taking up. At 9.15 am reocc. G.F. called + replied. Quiet until afternoon when considerable activity noted in every line + enemy commenced shelling INCHY & MOEUVRES about 5.30pm. At.P.I. S 4.5 pm SOS call received + SOS fired. Enemy counter-attacked + fire at SOS rate was kept up till about 7.30 pm. Enemy forwards + private. Attack was broken off + artillery fire in said "Than than their first change." Unexpected alarm messages from own SPD.A. wires about 9.30 pm on evidence of barrage overnight. JHL	2/L M. MEABURN Jan 26.7.85 of King's actg. Capt. 14.9.18
	13/9/18		Guns being dug in + depth against this outstanding. Four Jam Huns. Ken Corps German consolidated at 2 am. SOS line 28 Y83 brought in slightly. Quiet morning about 6 pm SOS. Comm. fired + reply. Re S. ft. + 28 Y83 hostile fired and two active batteries at hunt until 7.30 pm. There was no enemy action.	

WAR DIARY or INTELLIGENCE SUMMARY

Army Form C. 2118.

September 1918.   9th Bay and 274

Place	Date	Hour	Summary of Events and Information	Remarks and references to Appendices
PRONVILLE	14/9/18		And so far as can be ascertained the only reason for the SOS call was that the enemy who appeared to be bringing up LYNX TRENCH towards MOEUVRES. About 10.45 pm enemy trench mortars shelled Bayonet Cn in front, had been making considerable movement in the vicinity all day. Capt Capt HUGH WARNE was slightly wounded at is attributed from one of these shells. JAG	
	15/9/18 Sunday		Visited Pronjade OP & formed that line had been approached for about one mile by Royal Armoured Division. Reported am. LOCKWOOD's Coys roads supp. Enemy intermittent shelled Buttle Aveny all day & night. JAG	
			At 5.42 am SOS was sent on SOS have called for in response to enemy shelling of our front lines. Stopped about 6.20 am. Enemy fairly quiet during day except for some shelling of 50-B34 area about 2 pm. 155-23 & 1.32 etc about 170-B34 in right sector. 2/59 pnl cam. The gas cloud slid along night & early morning 9/16 in enemy deposits. Little heavy trench mortar cover from batteries.	
	16/9/18		Considerable aerial activity during night & early morning on our front. No enemy activity except during night when several bombing machines flew over. At 2.30 am 15.4.20 & B53 ordered to fire on SOS lines dispersing enemy as he got from rear reports captured. At 4.15 am three batteries again called to fire on CANAL DU NORD banks in Square E.15.C. as enemy believed to be massing there. About 8 pm enemy shelled area with persistence (4.2") containing 60% Gas to N.P. They made a direct hit on the Concrete post near by 14.735 kg an officers' mess and

WAR DIARY or INTELLIGENCE SUMMARY

Army Form C. 2118.

Place	Date	Hour	Summary of Events and Information	Remarks and references to Appendices
PRONVILLE	17/9/18	2am	Sergeant wounded No. 117437 Pearson GARSIDE afterwards died of his wounds. The officers kits were destroyed and all compiled stuff attached to present. W/BJs +20/185 from 7pm to 10-30pm Carrier and harassing fire to prevent enemy reaching & front line Canal during depth relief. 157 D.B. relieved 172 D.B. in left sector during night. Battery handed over our two head quarters + 9735= batteries this about 2am when a very heavy thunderstorm broke and swamped trenches & dugouts. Morning fine after the storm, having actually quiet throughout. Enemy artillery quiet. Troops reports wire coming over the crest after relief in large bodies. Hostilities the nose food. As far as can only ascertain that every gun pit were to provide for the line. 57th Div. Artly. were relieved by 40th Div. Arty yesterday. At 2.20pm received orders to reconnoitre position for one Brigade in sq'res D.29.c, positions being near the cemetery at short notice, guns kept standing to BADMUTE-CAMBRAI road. Took one battle commander at 4 p.m. to reconnoitre. No front position available, all probable positions being now occupied. On return at 7pm found this relief B.E.Q. had been relieved at 6.38 and SOS called for at 6.35 pm. Enemy heavily barraged MOEUVRES and wounded & attacked about 6.45pm. He was driven out of MOEUVRES but obtained one position from North gun. L.T.D.D.Q. UP-SUIT 5/169 85.pm. ended a hear & U.K. — —	
	18/9/18		Heavy rain about 3 am. At 2.20 am received warning line for 5/69 +25/185. Enemy artillery fairly active during day and about 5 p.m. put down barrage. After scouts of Division arms. The barrage extended F.R. North and at 5.30pm SOS was called for and kept up till about 7.30pm at varying rate. Chiefly slow, heavy bombardment by guns shell. 5/69 retaliated to at wire in square E. of MOEUVRES. as a two front barrage. 5/69 etc. position W of MOEUVRES and encrossed in SAY. At 5.30pm CRA 52 Div head	

WAR DIARY
INTELLIGENCE SUMMARY.

September 1918   9/43rd A/Bde

Place	Date	Hour	Summary of Events and Information	Remarks and references to Appendices
PRONVILLE	1/9/18		Continues at 5785'4 HQs and gave range & angle of proposed operation. On night 1/9/18 = 2/9/18 are to move to approx D29.c one mile NN of BOURSIES and the 15th debut until this operation commences. A/60 fired orientation shots during night in Cinquenhin with other batteries. Shifts on CANAL-DU-NORD line. 2 Lieut V.B. SMITH and H.M. BATES posts to brigade arrived at 5285.7490. & posts at W.P.28.C5.85.	A/L C
			Received orders that 53rd S.B. was in our position. At 11 am OC 286738 R-27th arrived to inspect position & survey details. At 2pm CRO 52nd D.A. arrived & gave details for a barrage. Bty carried out at 7pm by all batteries 9/9 28.30, 33.75.80, 17.8 & 78.1 when 9 MOEUVRES for recovery of MOEUVRES. The barrage began fired at 7 pm, 10 minutes later had 33 minute normal RMOEUVRES was carried At 8:15pm barrage commenced withdrawing from positions on arrival of 286 R-27th and moved to new position near BOURSIES. Battains took dd in by 1 am with no casualty. Brigade PC a short by w.	A/L C
BOURSIES	2/9/18		Battain ordered & reconnoitre proposals & commence registration. Being ordered support in vicinity of position. After nightfall enemy gassed battery areas and shelled same crossing a fire for casualties occurred wounding NO 82619 4th B/Bourne F.A & 52772 D. Gunner ROBERTSON G.W.	A/L C
	3/9/18		Reconnitred for OP's known new front which 52' D. is to take over for Grand Division. Vicinity of 13th 14th, shelled fairly heavily from about 2pm onwards. Registration received informing that 9/Bgde would form a 2nd group together with 93rd 96 R-27th which comes into action tomorrow night. Cinsiderable aerial activity in course by both had airplanes & 2 R/g Clasped. Fairly active bombing at night.	A/L C

Army Form C. 2118.

WAR DIARY
INTELLIGENCE SUMMARY.

of 92nd Bde R.F.A.   September 1918.

Place	Date	Hour	Summary of Events and Information	Remarks and references to Appendices
BOURSIES	22/9/18	2 a.m.	Received orders concerning Brigade units and arty & Bnrd's to become active. 25"Bty had a further ten gas casualties. Day fairly quiet but increasing enemy command shelling MOEUVRES and at 9.10pm SOS signal sent up. Batteries were shelled & communications with all batteries except one were severed. 92 Bde received 9 shorts shooting practice as spot. Ward, was in person & change it. Practice Ram SOS went up. 28"Bty had 7 casualties. Lieut 239454 Sunner McDONALD D., Wounded 68321 Bdr STEVENS W. 70586 B/R Gunner N, 52914 Gunner ALLISON R.A. 6757 Gunner ALLISON W. 57123 Bt. HUGHES H.A. 720973 & ING.R. Remains. Wright Ernest. 93 Bde HQ came into Boursies captured 7.7 Hows 2019 & 93 1/10490M	Bdr HANCOCK 202515 ASH LLEWIS 283185 & BEVER 315195 wounded & missing. Dubois Syts & miscap
	23/9/18		Report of enemy held MOEUVRES was being studied & an-OP Corner not completing this. Being relieved considered too. Enemy 90/16A 52"Bde visited Bde HQ and explained scheme & future operations. Enemy aircraft seemed vicinity of HQ. and bulletin areas but inflicted no casualties. MOEUVRES again shelled at night but no enemy action followed. JHA	Bt JAMES 5/9/18 B McRoberts 8/1/19 Lieut KNIGHT 20- R WARREN 19t ammunition hades & Bde VIII Corps. Ont Sgt* YORK 52 Div Bnd Bde coming 9/52.Obm
	24/9/18		Considerable artillery energy & improvement in weather. MOEUVRES again shelled from 3°45a.m. to 6.10 a.m. Rear quiet finish. Quiet except for enemy shelling of BOURSIES. Enemy hist ammunition dump near heavy battery 100+5 of Bde HQ, too gun balloon changes and in afternoon 4 enemy aircraft. JHA	
	25/9/18		SOS sent up on our left at 6 a.m. SOS called for by RIFA Brigade on our left & fired for 10 minutes & then stopped as there was nothing on our front. Wet & overcast in morning. Better when CO Generals received. Visits CRA 52 Div. in evening conversed. Quiet night. 201414 Cannoll 89267 & BRIGGS M4Y35" killed on return. JHA	
	26/9/18		Quiet day. Barrage maps received and other maps studied. 9"Bde Conv Operation of 157 Bde & Captain A map of portion of HINDENBURG line W of Canal du Nord & Roads of MOEUVRES. Arranged to join Opt 157 Bde at his HQs & act in liaison with him. JHA	

WAR DIARY / INTELLIGENCE SUMMARY

Army Form C. 2118.

9/13th R[oyal] F[usiliers]   September 1918

Place	Date	Hour	Summary of Events and Information	Remarks and references to Appendices

E. of MOEUVRES — **27/9/18**

Zero hour was 5:20 am. 9/13th barrage lasted 95 minutes & then stopped. Shelter trench N. of 157? 9/13th mopped up to South where Grenade Div. moved a few platoons N. towards BAPAUME-CAMBRAI road. A few parties of machine gunners were left behind to advance of artillery ordered to move & back first N. & parallel to BAPAUME-CAMBRAI road. 9/13th were in Brigade meanwhile with 2 battalions came into machine gun fire from front just E. of CAMBRAI-ARRAS? & Nord & to Canning line was imperative. Though enemy resistance and no hold up would exist, the expedition was reported & to one true & cross at MOEUVRES an approaching offensive forward movement & heard states when we were ordered to stop & come into action at forward operation to aid further positions 9/57°.84. On approaching K.9°.C.157? 9/13 came out and had no news before we continued movement. 20/157 got news first & came into action which 2 enemy batteries which had about average 1 obtained some forth onward shooting on enemy infantry and silenced an enemy 77 mm battery finally up on K.9/C. Cheringen 19?.128 & 9/69 Large 63°-S.C.A. & over. Batt. Comdrs. was told to form a ?? up to K.9/C 57-17? Large 63°-S.C.A. & over. That division. O. 57?/Div. forcing through 63° Div. K. CRA 57°.8'?
Orders from a Coll in the front ad did so, using it for SOS purposes t/for however, 63rd Div. have occurred GRAINCOURT & ANNEUX & 57° Div. we 7th? & served CANTAING line but failed to take Gr. Chapelle 8926? Prisoners BRIGGS & 15/S killed & 25 ?/K.

Army Form C. 2118.

WAR DIARY
INTELLIGENCE SUMMARY.

(Erase heading not required.)

9th Bn. R.D.F. September 1918

Place	Date	Hour	Summary of Events and Information	Remarks and references to Appendices
CANTAING	28/9/18		At 7am. the Bn. HQ at 63.d.8.8. at 63.b.8.8. the assistant war orderly. Offr. Bns. staby received orders to move to position E. of line GRAINCOURT-ANNEUX. Previous at 5.30 am at 7.30 am from a battery in support of 57th D. The incident in reaching CANTAING into it. 80 into action near ANNEUX about 12 noon & true the moved to move on a position near CANTAING which in gd held about 3 to 4 pm. 3/9/9/15. Carmichael Shell fire at the pourt of the advance he got through without casualty. Endeavord to getting a few targets, but the enemy got out of the valley through available Norwich and chiefly to seek for shelter to avoid our of the night. 28 & 19. batteries being harassed. Their positions were very few. Cas: Cas: harr. maps. Corporals 19185 64209 13th BIRCH Shells harr. 117510 Gr. BIGGS 14, 149835 S. GARNETT B. 82785 S. JUGG J. - Gunners. 9/69.185 122059 S. PIERCE W.S. killed D.G.g.	
	29/9/18		Heavy bomby a on left in morning. Key point and observations post but chased later on 4 battered. got some direct damages on retiring enemy 63.d.8.2. retired 57.6.5.2. 4 Convoys CANAL de L'ESCAUT. Every thin an G.S.R. shot about 12 men. killing N° 68091 dr.r.l Gilbert. H. 20.73.5 and wounding 2/Lt. O. MAY ERS and 176034 Sapt. MCROBERTS J. NH 4 10868 Sapt. LEE. Foo part. 3/69 N°3. Every opposed 1 RN Guernsey retiring about 11 am. ours drawn into Gattam opened on them as they retired E up slopes towards CAMBRAI - RUMILLY round getting one good target. 3/69 claim 8 hours hit a gun t 19.85 a G.S. wagon. About 12.30 pm. some heavy shell fell in 19.8.3. Drops Linda killing 6 & inj. S. GOODFELLOW. 57976 fr. LINDSY W.J. 68235.D. DAVIS + wounding 910930 S. ELGAR and killing 10 horses and wounding 7 & setting type to 4 wagon which in following extinguished by a Capt. M. MEABURN. Orr. in posit about 12.30 pm observed Ecart t Denmark.	

WAR DIARY / INTELLIGENCE SUMMARY

9th Bn RWF September 1918

Place	Date	Hour	Summary of Events and Information	Remarks and references to Appendices
			to get in touch but 2nd Div on Rgts were held up & their account a Gap on the lps of the 63rd Div. Large fires seen in CAMBRAI. heavy spasmodic shell'd valley during day. Artillery began G.P. Barrage about 4 P.M. but were held up at Crossings of CANAL de L'ESCAUT by heavy shrapnel and as came into action in the Valley. Quiet night. Showing further Casualties sustained 28"BN 54545 Sgt J. ROSS, 86093 Pte MASTERS A, 204710 Pte SHERWIN, 51018 Pte PEETE, 191515 Pte PAYNE T. 815407 Pte OTTWELL A. 203908 wounded 225783 Pte MORGAN W 65583 Pte HOLLINGSWORTH. Pte HAYDEN. E. GRAHAM 8th HAMPSTEAD wounded (at duty)	
CANTAING	30/9/18		63rd & 5th Div established S.W. of CAMBRAI. Artillery commencing to move in morning. being relieved night 9th ESCAUT. At 1pm fired a barrage in support of attack by 63rd Div. on trenches S.W. of CAMBRAI and on FAU. BOURG de PARIS. 19th BN. lost 7 more animals. Through enemy shell fire. Quiet night.	

S. Williams
Lt Col
Commdg 9th Bn RWF
1/10/18

Increase and Decrease for month of September 1918.

Increase.

Reinforcements		From Hospital		Remarks
Officers	O. Ranks	Officers	O. Ranks	
2.	84.	—	10.	Lieut. Bates. Lieut. R.W. Smith.

Decrease.

Killed		Wounded		To Hosp. (Cas.)		To Hosp. (Sick)		To U.K. for Commission	Remarks
Officers	O. Ranks	Officers	O. Ranks	Officers	O. Ranks	Officers	O. Ranks		
1.	10.	2.	43.	—	28.	1.	31.	2.	Major V.S. Longman. (Killed) 1-9-18. Lt. E.J. Kerridge. (Wounded) 1-9-18. Lt. F. Hawkes. (—) 30.8.18. Lt. G.R. Cook. (Sick) 24.9.18. 80813. Cpl. Galloway. G. } to U.K. 73384 " Hartland. G. }

D. Kerr.
Lieut: Col. R.A.
Comdg: 9ᵗʰ Brigade R.F.A.

1-10-18.

WAR DIARY / INTELLIGENCE SUMMARY

Army Form C. 2118.

9 Brigade R.F.A.   Oct 1918.

Place	Date	Hour	Summary of Events and Information	Remarks and references to Appendices
CANTAING	1/10/18		Heavy artillery fired to North from 5 am onwards. Title Report given. At 10.30 am received orders to send an officer reconnaissance across the CANAL de L'ESCAUT & take on strong points in front of infantry line. At 5.44 pm fired a barrage for 88 minutes in support of an attack by 152nd Bde. q 52.b.52. on Faubourg de PARIS. At 7 pm was called to Gp HQrs 2nd D.I. Tour & get teams up to be prepared to cross CANAL de L'ESCAUT during night & on reaching Divisional Reserve up at 10 pm. At 11.30 pm situation was still reserve. O/O	Major J Hickey Staff Captain from leave
	2/10/18		12.30 am was told that Brigade was to lift over area spent at dawn. Situation obscure in morning. Sent two Battery ammunition to reconnoitre for position for brigade front E of CANAL de L'ESCAUT as bridges my have to more there. Divisional orders 52.S.R. reference 63/SR. At 6.20 am B/Bg fired a concentration of 40 rounds on houses in South entrance of FAUBOURG de PARIS. During this bombardment Bd had a premature which killed No 152836 Gnr MILLMAN H, & wounded 61399 Sgt UBSDELL F.J. & 72737 Cpl O'NEILL P. Owing to heavy HE fire on teams was unable to obtain supplies this morning. Enemy not fire into area & truck in advance & on move over these positions. Batteries harassed FAUBOURG - de - PARIS & neighbourhood during day & night.	
	3/10/18		Our infantry reported there made a slight advance during night and other captured strong points S of CANTAING. This was subsequently found not to be. Remainder E of ESCAUT could be/Bg battery relieve & carried out their advance. Infantry received orders that not permissible to advance. By R/Balloon was asked for and shot sent out Zh there before 7.30 pm. At 4.30 pm called by CRA to conference & having arranged & received details to attack FAUBOURG de PARIS at 11 pm. 70/8S move teams down without incidents but there within Mg fire at times opposite when on barrage to unmade. Neighbourhood of bridge heavily shelled at night. O/O	
	4/10/18		Situation obscure, apparently no attack on the FAUBOURG de PARIS has had a complete success. We were 2nd relieved from battery positions, billets & wards & appeared to be doing very many shoots for an hrs GUENCHAY. At evening many shoots for an hrs GUENCHAY. 3/bg carried out own	

Army Form C. 2118.

WAR DIARY
INTELLIGENCE SUMMARY.

(Erase heading not required.) 9/BARDA

October 1918

Place	Date	Hour	Summary of Events and Information	Remarks and references to Appendices
CANTAING	5/10/18		Enemy artillery active throughout the night. At 5 am he put down a barrage on our front line & gradually approach reserves. In the morning he continued harass reserve areas & on heavier armed hostile recce. In front Shed Avenue & the with sniping. 19° & 20° Battn 67ᵗʰ had guns hit during the night. No casualties. Our sniper Major Orchard & Cᵒ behind Sqr L1 (Sheet 57BNW). 5/18A moved back for 3 days rest in front convent 7·9·9·5·4 org 20·18·5 arrived to recover Capt. Bangin [illegible] to take in our 2nd 6. transport owing to favourable terrain from German from South. At 7pm was sent for by CRA and took hgrs to bayou source the ESCAUT CANAL as soon as possible. At 8pm 2/19 crossed front line at 9.10pm L28 ± at 11 pm. Battalion got caught reserve but by firm foot took as many as twenty enemy and balloons from hit the rolls up the front was left where the West near MOYELLES were [illegible] located. But HQ opened 20/9/5 for the night. (awarded HQ Lint.)	Major PRINCE 2d Co previous line. Major SEABURNE attached F & S. 5/18A & Cᵒ [illegible] Stephens. Until time aerial from midnight 5/6? [illegible]
NE q. NOYELLES SUR ESCAUT	6/10/18		Remainder of 1920 moved across and took up position in [illegible] of between New Zealand Army (1st & 7th position just W. of 9/8/9/4/5/. Battalion lay by light. Received training. Enemy harass area all day but was not so active at night. Damages while in 19°·20° 18°·5 & a hurrying in. 9/69. [illegible] 52 4930. Came into action near NOYELLES & formed pump with 9/73 de. [illegible]	Lt MARSHALL. Act'g Co leave. His officer is a sergeant would ten leave to own [illegible] an OR vacancy.
— do —	7/10/18		Quiet night. Company with previously night. This dirt during in CAMBRAI. Enemy harass area with M.G fire periodically during night. At 7 am received his hearing for barrage. Kh fired & even howitzer 9/63 & NS. or Z day. Moorings badly received a definite backing to their fire in or Bourlois private such as cross roads to Bourlois and to [illegible] another 100 yds far from a/a barrage works and & 350 yds from town 'Caewell Malling 123st E MORGAN for the 8° - form here 4.30 am 8 1·37 pm receive orders others to the 8° - form here 4.30 am Thou return hid areas and adapted onto the Drapston Ridge leaving them with	

WAR DIARY
INTELLIGENCE SUMMARY.

Army Form C. 2118.

October 1918

Place	Date	Hour	Summary of Events and Information	Remarks and references to Appendices
Nr. NOYELLES	8/10/18		The 57th 93rd instead of bringing them on heavy shells N included 4.2"s with machine gun. No casualties. Things on our side pretty quiet prepart. JHe	Appendix A 6/10/18 from 0753 93rd
			Barrage commenced 4.30 am and continued for 3 hours 32 minutes. Line down to division & 93rd to most of the time. Barrage was in heavy right. We did hang but we put some around near the both positions & gas shells on H.Q. (mustard). Following casualties occurred. 19 93rd. Wounded Lt. C. MIDDLETON, 3955 S. SARSHAM J. – one gun injured. Inert question. 2895* killed 72991 Pte NATSON P. 265364 S. SCOTT R. 91304 S. KEMPT R. Wounded Capt. M.J. de KIRK 65424 Lt. D.Y. McLAGAN W.R. 211412 S. PASS J. - S. MARSTON (S. 23629 S. HODGSON. Art. Gun Ptl gnl question. 5 by all gun team front, points. Two further casualties occurred in 26 93rd. Sn. by running wounded. 209366 Sjt J. PUSHER 76702 S. MELLOWS. Active bombing of target areas by enemy planes McChadler in 9103d. Sepndrian. JHe	
SW CAMBRAI	9/10/18		From 5.25 am 18 Pdr batteries carried out a smoke barrage in conjunction with further advance of 63 division. On completion morning brigade was moved to R.S.E. GUYENCOURT and orders preceded hereafter during time. When it was necessary to advance to near N.E. GUYERGIES. t far N. JANCOURT on the outskirts of CAMBRAI. Brigade acted this in position of readiness for the later on orders to the artillery. Enemy shells were layed over in but caused little damage. Casualties 20: 26326 S. ISHERWOOD Wounded. JHe	
Nr. RIEUX	10/10/18		Brigade trekking at 5 am & arrived in parks to Captures NAVES. At 6.30 am received orders to advance to support infantry. Word brigade proceeded to 1st March with Northamptonshire Regt. I.O. 20.155 Nr. at action. Little opposition but some very energetic shelling by enemy from around on valley of afternoon.	

WAR DIARY of
INTELLIGENCE SUMMARY

Army Form C. 2118.

(Erase heading not required.)

G 15/4/1918 — October 1918

Place	Date	Hour	Summary of Events and Information	Remarks and references to Appendices
			Orders 28th L&Yorks into action to cover retirement of infantry. 16 MK ordered to immediately support infantry. Infantry retired assaulting battalion & most further assistance firing on which friends or foes unknown. AVESNES was captured. CRA then ordered brigade (at mercy of close support) to try to get into action N.E. of green. On reconnoitring it was found that the place was with a few hundred yards of enemy M.Gs and troops on our left had not got in to support. Therefore did not move the infantry commander cases it possible it difficult. Enemy fire active at mips & was not considered trying and any an Henry activity was not up and his aeroplanes over of. Enemy Aeroplanes very active in bombing tracks. Our 3 gun balloons. May Jas G. Qun planes up. Casualties 290541 D-SMITH F.S wounded 28 Yks, 240807 D-JAMES, 67864 D-GLENN 238214 F Cave S/69 all wounded	
nr. REUX	11/10/18		Brigade ordered 5th (next) troops to assist advance. 17 Sdy/568 attack on high ground N.W. of AUBERT. 17 Sdy attained 78°58' at 5.45 a.m. Infantry advanced opposite without opposition. AVESNES by lower barrage b own guns 4.30 a.m. Our Regard secured the objective but troops on our left were counter attacked with tanks & driven back a lot attempts to recover ground. Brigade ordered to search ground behind ridge from which enemy counter attacked at close rate for an hour. Casualties 746909 Signaller WENN. 550M D-BULING wounded 26425 L/9281 B.D CLINE wounded	

WAR DIARY or INTELLIGENCE SUMMARY

Army Form C. 2118.

(Erase heading not required.)

G.93 Bde RFA

October 1918

Place	Date	Hour	Summary of Events and Information	Remarks and references to Appendices
ST AUBERT	12/10/18		Ordered to follow 93rd Bde RFA which was moving in immediate support of infantry and to reconnoitre a position gun position about a mile N.E. GRIEUX. Arrived here at 10 am & waited till 1/15 for 93 DRFA to move. Then followed them. Ordered into action near HALLESSEN CAUCHERS. 93 Bde ordered at 3pm to move into position about 1½ mile N.E. of ST AUBERT. Bde. Commander Recomm and on way to position Bde Lieut on behalf of 157 Bde XVII Corps to take orders. It was moving to a dangerous locality & rapidly on our left & was not clear. It was consequently decided & agreed & get into position & find cover + at 6.30pm to support infantry. Attempt to cross R. SELLE near MONTECOURT. Infantry failed & failed to cover to hold on this platform gunnery forced to cross the SELLE & bridge was crumbled. Stark infantry visible on his all day but no support from to friend enemy shelly heights on to wait into action. It has turned a great effort into the valley in which it was state of position. 2/Lt 93 Bde had Shrove fever. Wounded & 197429. D. REES E. wounded.	
	13/10/18		Very Misty. HQ's were but not in a railway cutting just N of ST AUBERT & have shells out at 7.30 am by 5.9" shells which dropped 2 shells in the cutting Killing Nr. B17804 Gunner A.R. DELF M.M. 51/64 N.S. & Wounding Nr. 137177 Br. EDWARDS. 91132 H.Q. known to Bde. Orders further back & 500 yds for gun damages in position. Batteries reports during day. Visibility low. Very low in & 18 advance of infantry E. of R. SELLE. Enemy action most quiet. Action most quiet - air quiet. Bompts about deeper gun positions. A.R. heard his father field officers of med left. Officer strength & how live & the order of position of reinforcement.	

WAR DIARY
INTELLIGENCE SUMMARY

(Erase heading not required.)

G. Battery R.F.A.   October 1918

Army Form C. 2118.

Place	Date	Hour	Summary of Events and Information	Remarks and references to Appendices
			Quiet. The Gd. Ind'd OP duties. Reconnoitring party (Lieut. Drawer & other subs.) to telling in the younger officers. The bar and splendid throughout. No 49949 Gr WADE 28°B's acting as O.O'S. XXIth Bn Rifles. A very fifty night among cellars, very active on MONTRECOURT road. LOOK FOR THE SHELL Patrol in rehearsal for our barrage on our counter preparation ST AUBERT shelled with gas but not of my locality. Our attack alarm. R sent returned to section & Capt'n 3 geranium but could not be carried or with 2 men from Old positions. Gr 270 apr FITZGEORGE. Lt 73763 Gr HOWLETT R.A. 28°B's wounded.	89134 Br PENSER & others fifty many from gfm hit. Reported on 16-
ST AUBERT	14/10/18		Enemy adding active during early hours & morning but Quiet after dawn so say in clear & our drawing plans transient. It is Td hoped they hat pick up target later, as jolly from the prisoners left by the enemy they seem to very determined in his attempt at camouflage shown & have been made. A prisoner out in open fields a sunken roads & there is being a little of broken enemy ammunition. Accompanied CRA 52 D.O. around batteries in morning. Battery area shelled intermittently all day by 4.2" and 5 heavy casualties amongst. 19-BE No 63758 Sgt SMITH N° 61505 Br POTTER wounded 203685, N° 90706 R JENKINS W killed 73411 Br BROMLEY wounds 28°B's. 70050 R RANCLIFFE wounded 119348 Sgt. J WELSH (M.M) shell shock. Out night batteries area shelled with gas shell and S.9".	
	15/10/18		1st Lieut G.T MANN D.S.O. took over command 52°D.F.A from B. But A.D MUSGRAVE D.S.O & visited battery. Barrage table to Corr on operation by 72°Bde received. 119 Battery much shelled all day by guns firing first out of action and one other damaged. Enemy fired & counter preparation after dark.	
	16/10/18		Enemy artillery very active all night with H.E gas on Bath area and on ST AUBERT. At 5.10 am first barrage of 90 minutes in support of a minor operation by 72°B/Bde to secure bridgehead over	

Army Form C. 2118.

WAR DIARY
INTELLIGENCE SUMMARY.
(Erase heading not required.)

October 1918

G.W. Bujchel? Lt.

Instructions regarding War Diaries and Intelligence Summaries are contained in F. S. Regs., Part II. and the Staff Manual respectively. Title pages will be prepared in manuscript.

Place	Date	Hour	Summary of Events and Information	Remarks and references to Appendices
			Ptes R. JELLE, N. SHEPPARD, N. KEALE & E. SHORES, battalions carried out task the two latter leaving their objectives & crossing about 200 prisoners. N. Shops were led 1/2 miles right forward. Continued forward advance in some time after it was dues & kept on advancing very slowly. L/Cpl. BCS came up in command & had Lt. N° 4 gun his killing. N° 66120 Cpl. GLEESON. M. 65791 B. DONNETT C.H. 263308 R. COMPTON 62/3/8 SLATER M153 R. RIGG J. and wounding M° 36072 R. BEATTIE. J. and turning out Pte Gun. 28° Batt. had some ammunition left & all batteries were forced to go on nest at night. Sgt. BATES 28°BG Cpl SOWER 28°BG Cpl. SHEPPARD. Following day enrolled 18 R. STANTON J. 270173 R. PEPPER 28°BG. 26 BN 24°BG POWER N 5/28°B1. R. TRUTH recruiting sgt. 28°BG the others Lt. BATES a few fine & new MONTRECOURT took & rush kit bauble of Lt Gel at Cpl of the casualties the Sgt & forward during the house, gunshipe. Sgt. Sowers to retiring from Sunny Bigot was damaged & kept & action from H. V. Shell Lt had trench-break pneumonia of his practice of 19°BS which agreed ordeas him Zone. 19°BS next present position smith. Received intelligence that everyone here to retain on night 17/18°. Reports stated BOROVILLE- en-ROULX for the very area
ST AUBERT	17/10/18		Summary rather peaceful at night. Opt Leroy Christmas all yesterday. On in funk went here to Gel S.O.S liaison but the others. 19°BS had severe casualties & Their wagon line during after noon 4 OR's following being killed 68284 Sally WHEELER G.N 35 B.St. WILSON + wounded 384635 B. WILLIS. J.N 91685 B. TOWEY. D. 15596 D. FALCONER N. 97788 D. FITZGERALD. J. 129100 S. MATTHEWS. J.E. Others Hqs wounded & Command. 19°BS Killed	

Army Form C. 2118.

WAR DIARY
or
INTELLIGENCE SUMMARY.

(Erase heading not required.)

9/13 A R F A

October 1918

Instructions regarding War Diaries and Intelligence Summaries are contained in F. S. Regs., Part II. and the Staff Manual respectively. Title pages will be prepared in manuscript.

Place	Date	Hour	Summary of Events and Information	Remarks and references to Appendices
ST AUBERT	17/10/18		5/69 also reports following casualties which occurred on afternoon of 16th inst - Lieut R.T. WORSWICK & Lieut W WEED from Bomber N°. 212973. St PERNICOTT. 105754 & Bomb D. 65935 A CHAMBERS. F. 141150 & Lieut A. KEITH A and three runners killed. These men were employed by 20th & 25th Divs which were being relieved. 28/B35 had opened fire from 72nd Battery but in order to conserve position as being in ridge. The morning divided their fire and the shell did not do damage. Nor the gun could not be moved. At 5.0pm 5/69 casualties from H.Q. were relieved at 5.30pm. Marched via SPIESNES-CAMBRESIS (Province) arriving 9.30pm. 4/63 Div arrived 9.30pm & 14 2/45 at 10.15pm. 20/B35 around 11.30pm & 28/L had left midnight. The 5/69 left 1.0AM. Paced in with Divisions and several casualties from it 14/B35. on passing through AVESNES-LE-SEC had to take wounded N°. 584485 Sgt HOLLAND A and N°. 37093 Cpl McNICHOL S. J. 28/B35 had Lieut a similar position as being (5) lamp, it and 8 others wounded. The piece was highly bury in a 4 bay kitchen... his wounded were comestible to the front until later the... wounded was wounded...	Lt WORSWICK ex 52/35 T.M. B5. Lt WEED from 52/35 T.M. B5. attached to Bn for half 5/69 28/ B5.
PROVILLE nr CAMBRAI.	18/10/18		Nothing of note. Brigade received orders to march tomorrow to MORCHIES area & entrain at VELU & FREMICOURT or ACQ TECURE.	high SF Borne arrived 22/35
	19/10/18		Marched at 11 am. Strong 36 1/3 with via ESMAKELIENS. CANTAING, FONTAINE-NOTRE DAME and CAMBRAI. BAPAUME and &MORCHIES arriving 4.30pm. Orders for entraining received at 11.30pm.	
MORCHIES	20/10/18		Very cold night also. 16/B35 moved VELO at 8 am & entrain. left train station at 12.15. 20/B35 start 15.15, 28/B35 15.45, 5/69 at 15. ANTB M HRS at OO15. soon after leaving camp 5/69 drove	

Army Form C. 2118.

WAR DIARY
or
INTELLIGENCE SUMMARY.
(Erase heading not required.)

9.2.3 M.R.D.A.   October 1918

Place	Date	Hour	Summary of Events and Information	Remarks and references to Appendices
			After a short shell or else a stick bomb trap and 8 men were severely wounded & 9 men killed. It was raining hard at the time and the road was deep in mud & casualties were very bad. The men cleared the whole scene although so lately wounded, two men had their legs blown off. The fractures suffered to Mainly a Motor ambulance were soon procured, parts of the Ambulance of the driver & Coml. The (unfortunate) Stretcher bearers & men wounded in this work, their names Were 11793 Pte BINGHAM F, 101572 A/Sgt. McFRASER, 23367 Pte MATTHEWS H, 95442 WBR HUDSON LW 32626 Sgt PALFREEMAN A 145898 D. FEARNLEY, F 12137 D. SCOTT N 30087 D. KEENAN P. Mess Grenade left camp 9.0 pm, I arrived at station from 5/69 delays owing to the rail most. 5/69 continued left about midnight.	
ECURIE	21/10/18		Train for H.Q. 4rd Battn of 52 DHC arrived about 12:30 am & was loaded & we left & we got away till about 4.00 am passing through ACHIET-LE-GRAND at 6 am then to WINTON 5/69 which was entrainined. Arrived at ECURIE about 9 am. I hurried R.camp at MASSA GASCAR Comm. 19:-120-,28°,035 LYBOROW in camp. 5/69 and not yet in the camp till 4 pm. 321 LYDSON 28 185 proceed on leave.	

WAR DIARY
INTELLIGENCE SUMMARY

Army Form C. 2118.

(Erase heading not required.)

of **9 Sqdn RAF** October 1918

Place	Date	Hour	Summary of Events and Information	Remarks and references to Appendices
ECURIE	22/10/18		Units endeavoured to get to places thus stands made up the field cushion. It was arranged to bring cars fit for use of Army in the field to move on SOCKX 12th Army units began in afternoon	
	23/10/18		All guns stripped, hose kit and workshop, sent to PETEWAWA range of calibration. Orders to move tomorrow received. March at 8 a.m. HENIN-LIETARD area.	
COURCELLES LES-LENS	24/10/18		Marched at 8 a.m. - 57th Army history followed by 19, 20, 28. CAISNE were marched via SOUCHEZ, LIEVIN, LENS & HENIN-LIETARD. Arrived at letter place Brigade train arrived to move on to COURCELLES. Arrived 4 p.m. Total march about 18 miles. 56 & 79th billets at AUBY & 52 Sqdn & HQ at COURCELLES. This village has not been greatly damaged but a number of villains & horses have been found & murders for hyena have been opened about. Lt. R.J. MURFEY 20°/85 proceeds on leave. Lt MARSHALL A.V.C. reports from leave.	
	25/10/18		Parties to get touch with ordnance who had been ordered to deliver clothing which the men are much in need of. Their god kits also report mislaid. An enemy received orders for Brigade to move march to NAZIERS tomorrow following SS 15th.	
	26/10/18		Marched at 9.45 a.m. for NAZIERS via AUBY, FLERS, DOUAI - 19 SS leading /Hand	

WAR DIARY
INTELLIGENCE SUMMARY

Army Form C. 2118.

October 1918

Place	Date	Hour	Summary of Events and Information	Remarks and references to Appendices
WAZIERS	27/10/18		By S/69, 28ᵗʰ & 29ᵗʰ DAS. Ammn shot from cars billets in WAZIERS which is very badly damaged. Just N of WAZIERS Brigade was inspected by hopeful MARSHALL-CORNWALL. 52ⁿᵈ DAC Battn. had no has had much opportunity of cleaning up of the shortage of men & clothing renders the turnout poor.	SLC
	28/10/18		No firing heard. C.O. GOC RA & VIII Corps troops Brigade and inspected reports billets. 35 horses & 16 mules received in reinforcements distributed. DAM inspected firing of Brigade & ordered them to be fell. Batteries. Remainder of Brigade are in fair order.	SLC
			SAPPERS inspected animals and expressed himself pleased at their condition after the strenuous time they had been through. Major S.F. BURNE was ordered for next Senior officers course commencing Shorncliffe Nov 3ʳᵈ. Lt. MARSHALL AVC attended & spoke informally.	SLC
	29/10/18		Capt. G.H. ELLIOT joined Brigade from Reinforcement Camp and was posted to 28ᵗʰ Battery. Lecture was given by Capt. Morrison on the Stokes Mortar gun.	
	30/10/18		C.O. and B.C.'s went by lorry to 277 Army Bde. R.F.A in action near NIVELLE, with a view to relieving them for the action journey they suffered at brand, Pte. R.E.A, in MAGPIE, FORTUNE was given by Lt. GOURLAY on his experiences in prison in Germany. DMS	
	31/10/18		Lt.-Col. COTTER proceeded on leave to U.K. with Lt. Col. SOWLER (Veterinary) and Bdsm. Ramsay, 52ⁿᵈ D.A.C. Major S.F. BURNE took over command of Brigade. Orders received	

Army Form C. 2118.

WAR DIARY
or
INTELLIGENCE SUMMARY.
(Erase heading not required.)

94th Brigade R.F.A.

October 1918

Place	Date	Hour	Summary of Events and Information	Remarks and references to Appendices
WAZIERS	31/10/18		To march and return 12nd Bde. R.F.A. in 3rd pot. Major H.P. MORGAN joined Brigade from A/243 Army Brigade R.F.A. and was sent to 28 M. Battery vice Major BURNE, who was appointed Brigade Major 57th Divisional Artillery. A. Matche. Capt. R.F.A. for O.C. 94th Brigade R.F.A. 4th November 1918.	

CONFIDENTIAL 9S8

WAR DIARY

OF

9th Brigade R.F.A.

From 1/4/18. To 30/11/18

VOLUME

Army Form C. 2118.

WAR DIARY
or
INTELLIGENCE SUMMARY.

(Erase heading not required.)

94th Brigade R.F.A.   November 1918.

Place	Date	Hour	Summary of Events and Information	Remarks and references to Appendices
WAZIERS	1.11.18		Major S.F. BURNE, D.S.O. left Brigade to take up duties of Brigade Major 52th Division (Whitley). Major J. HICKEY assumed command of the Brigade. Orders received to send advance parties to neighbourhood of SAMEON, on 2nd inst.	
do	2.11.18		Nil	
do	3.11.18		Proceeded to billets in vicinity of SAMEON, 202th Position leading. Brig. Gen. WARD, unofficially inspected Brigade at ORCHIES. 3pm.	
do	4.11.18		Major A.H.N. HOUSE assumed command of Brigade. Brigade relieves 277th Army Brigade RFA in action near MONT-BU-PRÉY and NIVELLE. Night harassing fire carried out. 3pm.	
NIVELLE	5.11.18		B.G., R.A., 52nd Division visited Batteries and Brigade H.Q. Night harassing fire carried out. Brigade under direct orders of 52nd D.A. 3pm.	
do	6.11.18		Orders to be ready to move as enemy were expected to retire during night. A night harassing fire provided. An action of 192nd and one of 29th Brigade taken to assist Brigade to C.R.A. to clean up no show. Gen. WARD visited Bde. H.Q. 3pm.	
do	7.11.18		All Guns and wagons at full positions ready to move at two hours. Orders received about 0800 and teams sent back to wagon lines. 3pm.	
do	8.11.18		Informed about 0800 hours that Germans had gone. All batteries ordered to forward positions (except 14th) in accordance with orders previously received from 52nd D.A. 3pm.	
do 3pm. HARCHIES	9.11.18		Brigade advanced in support of 157 Infantry Division, across JARDCANAL and ANTOING CANAL and billeted for the night in HARCHIES. 3pm.	

1.

Army Form C. 2118.

WAR DIARY
or
INTELLIGENCE SUMMARY.

(Erase heading not required.)

9th Brigade R.F.A.   November 1918.

Instructions regarding War Diaries and Intelligence Summaries are contained in F. S. Regs., Part II. and the Staff Manual respectively. Title pages will be prepared in manuscript.

Place	Date	Hour	Summary of Events and Information	Remarks and references to Appendices
HAR. 3/11. VACRESSE	10.11.18		Brigade moved from HAROTIES to SIRHAUT via HAUTRAGE. The 29th Battery was detached to support 117 H.L.I. in their advance South of BOIS DE BAUDOUR and came into action in TERTRE and BOUDOUR. On the arrival of the remainder of the Brigade the 20th Battery put H guns in action at SIRHAUT, and sent 2 sections forward with the infantry to HERCHIES, where they were joined by the remainder of the battery in the evening. 19th Battery and D/14 Battery were billeted in SIRHAUT. 9h5	
"	11.11.18		19th and D/14 Batteries advanced to the station and occupied positions in the vicinity of VACRESSE to support the advance of the 157 Infantry Brigade at 7 A.M. Orders received not to fire after 11.00 a.m.	
"	12.11.18		At VACRESSE. Also 2nd Lt. J.R.W. COLLETT joined the Brigade and proceeded to 20th Battery.	
"	13.11.18		do. do.	
"	14.11.18		do. do.	
"	15.11.18		D/14 Took part in Infantry cavalry to A.D.M.S. by Army Commander. 9h5	
"	16.11.18		Nil. H.Q. returned to Very few for orderly awards from 13th Division. 9h5	
"	17.11.18		Parties from all Batteries and I.R. attended Divisional Thanksgiving service.	
"	18.11.18		Major B.N. HOWE attached to this Brigade heading over command of 9th Brigade to Major J. HICKEY R.F.A. at Col COTTER on return from leave, M.B. over all the of CRA in the absence of Brig-Gen MAIR on leave. 9h5	

2.

Army Form C. 2118.

WAR DIARY
or
INTELLIGENCE SUMMARY.

(A/2th Brigade R.F.A.) November 1918.

Place	Date	Hour	Summary of Events and Information	Remarks and references to Appendices
VACRESSE	19.11.18		A.M. Training cleaning guns	
do	20.11.18		do do	
do	21.11.18		do do	
do	22.11.18		do do	
do	23.11.18		194th Battery took part in a practice ceremonial Parade with 152nd Infantry Brigade near MAISIERES.	
do	24.11.18		A.M. Training and cleaning guns	
do	25.11.18		do do	
do	26.11.18		do do	
do	27.11.18		Competition for decoration for Smartness held. Improving and cleaning guns	
do	28.11.18		Training	
do	29.11.18		do	
do	30.11.18		do	

J. Mitchelon Capt. R.F.A.
Adjt A/2th R.F.A. 3/12/18.

Army Form C. 2118.

WAR DIARY
or
INTELLIGENCE SUMMARY.
(Erase heading not required.)

9th Brigade R.F.A.   November 1918.

Place	Date	Hour	Summary of Events and Information	Remarks and references to Appendices
WAZIERS	1.11.18		Major S.F. BURNE, D.S.O. left Brigade to take up duties of Brigade Major 57th Division. Whilst Major J. HICKEY assumed command of the Brigade. Orders received to send advance parties to neighbourhood of SAMEON on 2nd /11	
"	2.11.18		Marched to billets in vicinity of SAMEON, both Batteries finding Bde H.Q. were originally inspected Brigade at ORCHIES /11	
"	3.11.18		Major A/H A HOUSE Assistant Commander of Brigade. Brigade relieves 2/11 Army Brigade R.F.A. in neighbourhood of MONT-DU-PRÉ and NIVELLE. Night harassing fire carried out. /10	
NIVELLE	5.11.18		B.C.s & B.C. Parties recond Batteries and Brigade H.Q. Night harassing fire carried out. Brigade moved ahead area of SENS-A /11	
"	6.11.18		Ordered to be ready to move as enemy was reported to believe during night. Night harassing fire provided. On return of WR and on 7.15 A.M. orders issued to begin at once to clear up our front. (Gun ward) visited Bde H.Q. 3PM.	
"	7.11.18		A.C. Teams and Wagons etc got up and stood ready to move at two hours orders received about 1030 and teams sent back to wagon lines /11	
"	8.11.18		Support afforded those that Germans had got till batteries were in pursuit. Batteries (except 147) in readiness with Public Pursuit Mechanism from 9am. D.A.C.	
9am 9.11.18			Brigade advanced in support of 167 Infantry Brigade across JARDENAL and ANTOING CANAL and billed for the night in HARCHIES. /11	
HARCHIES				

WAR DIARY
or
INTELLIGENCE SUMMARY.

Army Form C. 2118.

9th Brigade R.F.A. November 1918.

Place	Date	Hour	Summary of Events and Information	Remarks and references to Appendices
VACRESSE	10.11.18		Brigade retreated from HARCHIES to SIRHAUT via HAUTRAGE. The 28th Battery was detached to support 17 H.L.I. in their advance south of BOIS DE BAUDOUR. On this action the remainder of the Brigade and the 26th Battery put up guns in action at SIRHAUT, and sent a section forward to the support of E HERCHIES, when they were driven by the remainder of the Battery in the morning. 18th Battery and D/4 Battery were billeted in SIRHAUT.	
"	11.11.18		18th and D/4 Batteries advanced before dawn, and occupied positions in the vicinity of VACRESSE to support the advance of the 157 Infantry Brigade at 7 am. Orders received not to fire after 11.0 am.	
"			At VACRESSE. All 2 /6 IRW COLLETT joined the Brigade and reported to OC Bty 9th.	
"	12.11.18		do. do.	
"	13.11.18		do. do.	
"	14.11.18		D/4 took part in offensive Battery to march by Army Commander DIC	
"	15.11.18		Mr. WD Reinmark of very pro quality received from 112th Division. All Service from all Batteries and the ordinary Divisional Thanksgiving service	
"	17.11.18			
"	18.11.18		Margaritt A HOUSE returned to his Battery having been concerned with the Brigade. Major J STUKLEY R.F.A. Lt. Col. CUTTER on return from leave took over the two 9 CRA on the absence of Brig. Gen. MAIR on leave etc.	

2

Army Form C. 2118.

WAR DIARY
or
INTELLIGENCE SUMMARY.
(Erase heading not required.)

A/M Brigade R.F.A.   November 1918

Place	Date	Hour	Summary of Events and Information	Remarks and references to Appendices
MORESEE	19.11.18		A.M. Drawing & cleaning 2/hr.	
do	20.11.18		do do 2/hr	
do	21.11.18		do do 2/hr	
do	22.11.18		do do 2/hr	
do	23.11.18		W/M Battery took part in approaching ceremonial Parade with 151st Infantry Brigade near ABISTERES. 2/hr	
do	24.11.18		All Drawing & cleaning 2/hr	
do	25.11.18		do do 2/hr	
do	26.11.18		do do 2/hr	
do	27.11.18		Competition for Chargewhen for Stabilised hut Drawing and cleaning 2/hr	
do	28.11.18		Continued do 2/hr	
do	29.11.18		do 2/hr	
do	30.11.18		do 2/hr	
			Mulan Capt. R.F.A.	
			Capt. A/M R.F.A. 31/11/18.	

Vol 9

CONFIDENTIAL
WAR DIARY
OF
9TH BRIGADE R.F.A

From 1/12/18 To 31/12/18

(Volume 12.)

Army Form C. 2118.

WAR DIARY
or
INTELLIGENCE SUMMARY.

9th Brigade R.F.A. December 1918.

Place	Date	Hour	Summary of Events and Information	Remarks and references to Appendices
WACRESSE	1.12.18		In Billets. 9M.	
do	2.12.18		Each 18 Pdr. Battery visited by a Company of 3d K.O.L.I. from 157 Infantry Brigade & lectures on shipping by an officer of R.A.F. 9M.	
do	3.12.18		Each 18 Pdr. Battery visited by a Company of 3d K.O.L.I. from 157 Infantry Brigade 9M.	
do	4.12.18		D/HQ visited by a party of 36 Officers from 157 Infantry Brigade 9M.	
do	5.12.18		Each 18 Pdr. Battery visited by a Company of 3d K.O.L.I. from 157 Infantry Brigade. Lt-Col. W.P. Grier. C.I.E. D.S.O. returned from acting C.R.A. and took over command 9M.	
do	6.12.18		Each 18 Pdr. Battery visited by a Company of 3d K.O.L.I. from 157 Infantry Brigade. Adjutant reported to S.C.R.A. and visited neighbourhood of THIEUSIES to see suitable places for Brigade to billet 9M.	
	-			
do	7.12.18		do 9M	
do	8.12.18		do 9M	
do	9.12.18		do 9M	
do	10.12.18		do 9M	
do	11.12.18		do 9M	
CASTEAU	12.12.18		Headquarters, 19th Battery and H/HQ Batteries marched - headquarters to CASTEAU and the two Batteries to THIEUSIES. 20th and 28th Batteries did not move. 9M	
do	13.12.18		In Billets 9M -	

Army Form C. 2118.

WAR DIARY
or
INTELLIGENCE SUMMARY.
(Erase heading not required.)

Instructions regarding War Diaries and Intelligence Summaries are contained in F. S. Regs., Part II and the Staff Manual respectively. Title pages will be prepared in manuscript.

Place	Date	Hour	Summary of Events and Information	Remarks and references to Appendices
CASTEAU	14.12.18		In Billets &c.	
do	15.12.18	do	28th Battalion moved into CASTEAU. &c.	
do	16.12.18	do	do	
do	17.12.18	do	20th Battalion moved into SIREUX. &c.	
do	18.12.18	do	do	
do	19.12.18	do	do	
do	20.12.18	do	do	
do	21.12.18	do	Brigade inspected by Divisional Commander in Drill Ground. &c.	
do	22.12.18	do	do	
do	23.12.18	do	Revd. SEMPLE leaves Brigade on Egypt. &c.	
do	24.12.18	do	do	
do	25.12.18	do	do	
do	26.12.18	do	do	
do	27.12.18	do	do	
do	28.12.18	do	do	
do	29.12.18	do	A/Capt H.H. NAISHE, Adjutant, left unit under orders to report for Indian's Office at	
do	30.12.18	do	do. A/Lt. Carpenter reports suppose admitted. Coal mines commenced dumping 7, 16 morning	
do	31.12.18	do	do. A/Capt. C. Cadman called for 11. T.E. men over than serving in before 11.11.19. Also 4 20	
			† known as WATFORD district and home this day.	

† A7093. W: W1223 9/M1293 750,000. 1/17. D: D & L. Ltd. Forms/C2118/14.

Army Form C. 2118.

WAR DIARY
or
INTELLIGENCE SUMMARY.
(Erase heading not required.)

9th Brigade R.F.A.   Appendix K Indian – Dec 1918

Place	Date	Hour	Summary of Events and Information	Remarks and references to Appendices

			Following are the Brigade armament billeting headquarters through 21st Div – 52 STA on Dec 68 d/27/12/18. 20 BR S/Sjt H.F. WYATT. 4135 S/Sgt G.D. MACKAY R.H. P. MORGAN
			D/69 45312 Sgt F.H. PIKE. 28 BR 25704 Sgt W. WATSON
			10336 Cpl J.H. POPKINS. 5399 Dr T. M. PEVERIL
			5084 Cpl T. COOK
			5690 Gr. R. McCULLOCH 631043 Dr R.S. LEYS
			
			Officers serving with Brigade on 31.12.18.
			HQ 19 D.A.M.
			Lt Col H.I. COTTER. C/E D/SO RGA DE. Capt (a/major) A.N. SMYTHE MC Lieut (a/major) LC.N. PRITCHARD Gads(a/major) H.P. MORGAN
			M/Maj H.A.H. WALSH. RFA adjutant 2/Lieut (Capt) M. MEABURN A/Capt E.C.H. ALLISON Capt L.3 LLOYD
			2 Lt HE. STANLEY. RFA Reconnaissance Officer Lieut R.H. ENGLEFIELD Lieut R.C.J. ALLISON Lieut T. BECKER
			Lieut H. SOWYER RFA (7) [illegible] 2/Lieut A.H. MALCOLM Lieut R.H. MOFFEY AJ ROSS
			M.O. J. MUNN. U.S.A. M.R.C. medical officer ” R. SMITH 2/Lt L.W. JUDD 2/Lt J. LYNTON
			Capt E. JACKSON RAMC R/S officer ” J.R.W. COLLETT ” R. NORRIS M.C. attached from
			    D/69 B5 4.5" How ” W.A. WHITTAKER Capt W EBB 52 STA.T/M.B.
			    Capt (a/major) J. HICKEY
			    Lieut (a/capt) W. WOOD
			    Lieut A.T.W. POWELL
			    2/Lt W.S.H. WINSHIP
			    ” A. ANDERSON
			    Lieut E.H. COLE attached from 52 Div T.M.B.
			
			Following Warrant & non-commissioned Officers in Brigade of 31/12/18. were awarded and promoted. No 68 / 12
			Lieut Colonel A.J. COTTER. C/E. D.S.O.
			N°1940 R.S.M. E.G. MARSHALL. RFA
			
			[signature]
			Lieut Col comdg 9 RFA RFA	

Confidential   Original

War Diary

9th Brigade R.F.A.

From   1st January 1919

To   31st January 1919

Vol I/1919.

WAR DIARY
or
INTELLIGENCE SUMMARY.

Army Form C. 2118.

(Erase heading not required.)

9 Brigade RFA January 1919

Place	Date 1919	Hour	Summary of Events and Information	Remarks and references to Appendices
CASTEAU Belgium 10 kilos N of MONS	Jan 1st		9 Card mines despatched to Reception Camp MONS for demobilisation. Lt Gnl Sir A HUNTER WESTON KCB MP passed through here and gave men of 9th RFA who had served with him or GALLIPOLI.	File
	Jan 2nd		10 Candidates despatched for demobilisation. Notice re demobilisation of students received.	File
	Jan 3rd		4 Candidates despatched for demobilisation. Guns offered 6 rounds completed. Demolition Strength of Brigade 410 horses 226 mules.	File
	Jan 4th		Officers ride held. Explanatory lecture by Bde Cdr on "Duties of probationers and methods of instruction." Two lorries tank parties to BRUSSELS placed at disposal of Bde now to relieve 10 Bty & 19 & 20 13.5's & 6 mm howitzers & Continuous despatches for demobilisation. Two rifles then despatch rider was concerned	File
	Sunday Jan 5th		Demobilisation cancelled P.727 received — The candidates relieves of men were not to go today. 6 mines detained by yesterday were ordered to go today.	File
	Jan 6th		6 Candidates detained & forward home for demobilisation. This Army mounts were allotted to Bdy ado to Bde parties from 6 RGA, Jan 28 RFA, Jan 28 RFA have now got their tomorrow.	File
	Jan 7th		Harness ordered for demobilisation. Divisional Artillery paraded for instruction regarding Jan ad port particulars that of 28 RFA which was standard passed. Capt HA H MARCH A adjutant	

Army Form C. 2118.

Instructions regarding War Diaries and Intelligence Summaries are contained in F. S. Regs., Part II. and the Staff Manual respectively. Title pages will be prepared in manuscript.

WAR DIARY
or
INTELLIGENCE SUMMARY.
(Erase heading not required.)

G.B. R.G.A.   January 1919.

Place	Date	Hour	Summary of Events and Information	Remarks and references to Appendices
CASTEAU	Jan 8th		Returned from interview at W.O. & R.A. ENGHEFIELD 14738. Recommended in charge of port special train to ENGLAND. Upon expiration of leave. Capt E.CH. ALBAN 20 "B" detailed for Brit ammunition barge at SHOEBURYNESS (said on 10th from ROUBAIX). Lieut R.J. MORSEY detailed to proceed to join 24th S.A. Siege COLOGNE as German speaking officer.	S/L
	Jan 9th		Following arrival in connection with New gun & ammunition armament William Crews. Dieu (Acpo) H.H.H. WALSHE. Ordnance Sergt M.T. 4441 Private V. MAGUIRE 28"B" R.G.A.	S/L
			One cool miner demobilised. Lt (Acpo) H.H.H. WALSHE M.C. left prolonged a leave of Embarkation ? men of three groups also experience for mobilisation. Divisional parade held at 10am in hurry train for presentation of arms of M.M. & M.S.M. to ACCO & men of the R.A. over 157 & B.G. Troops present were: Base of E.S.T.C. & C.O.C.O., D.D. H.Q., 157 & Ap B.G. (1/5 & 1/6 & 1/7 How.). Troops marched past and then dispersed. R.A. turn out very poor. Particulars 28"B" 35.	S/L
	Jan 10th		8 men gunners, 4 nom Drivers forwarded for demobilisation. Tobacco Lecture by Rev. GREENLAND, Esq to 56 R.A. 1 Gunner left on Dustman. Two pianos (12" & 30" see ans) sent to cultivation by motor lorry.	S/L
	Jan 11th		13 men - 10 Cooks arrived, 1 on 28 days leave (group 56) 1 forwarded with men of 100 m H.A. forward for demobilisation. They swing to truck about demobilisation orders have been received they all men proceed home on leave. Free from to improvement that they are to return at the expiration of their leave.	S/L

Army Form C. 2118.

WAR DIARY
~~or~~ INTELLIGENCE SUMMARY.
(Erase heading not required.)

of 9/1 B Sig Qtrs.   January 1919

Instructions regarding War Diaries and Intelligence Summaries are contained in F. S. Regs., Part II. and the Staff Manual respectively. Title pages will be prepared in manuscript.

Place	Date	Hour	Summary of Events and Information	Remarks and references to Appendices
CASTEAU	12 Jan		8 men proceeded on demobilisation. Company is now 100 under strength & will in consequence have had part to keeping horses, harness &c in good order. JHE	
	13 Jan		5 men proceeded on demobilisation. Lt R. J. MOTLEY proceeded to England in stead of Capt Gilmore (7152050) & per 27th Jan to in stead of Lt GR. 20th Battn. arrival letter from SIRIEUX to BASSE CASE armed 28th January by No 3 (SW) Section BHQ 52nd Div. Veterinary board classified remounts of HQ 28th January for retention or disposal. JHE	Major SMITHERS
	14 Jan		6 men proceeded for demobilisation. Veterinary board resumed classification of horses & mules, Cross Country Run in connection with sports 22nd Corps. Rowley 12 Sitartn. JHE	
	15 Jan		3 men proceeded for demobilisation. JHE	
	16 Jan		Lt ATW POWELL RFA B/84 B 1/2 proceeded on demobilisation. WO & NCOs proceeded on demobilisation per arr of Corps Commander in 18 and 19 JHE	
	17 Jan		9 men of 9/1 B.S. and 8 men of 9/14/56 B.S. Rendezvous had a Board for admission into RQ4 HQ. JHE	
	18 Jan		Command Parade for XXII Corps Commander for presentation of DCM ribbons - formerly LEMON B/64 & Sgt RIDLEY 1/1 B/64 received the ribbons. Letter to acknowledgement from the relatives of Staudert & No 492 Gunr. WM, No 60752 Sgt SMITH of men killed while service handed out.	

Army Form C. 2118.

Instructions regarding War Diaries and Intelligence Summaries are contained in F.S. Regs., Part II. and the Staff Manual respectively. Title pages will be prepared in manuscript.

WAR DIARY
or
INTELLIGENCE SUMMARY.
(Erase heading not required.)

9? BOURRA   January 1919.

Place	Date	Hour	Summary of Events and Information	Remarks and references to Appendices
	Sunday 19 Jan		Capt Cameron now pleased to remark that the turnout of the Revue actually was very good featured that of the battery (28ᵈ). *DGE*	9.30 to Bands SQRFC 1-0 m Divisional Platoon Competition
CASTEAU			Major J. HICKEY Officiating RA.BMRA. Capt v JARROTT on leave. *DGE*	Try finer — pumping pits Heavy wiper 11.45-12.45 Light wipe 9 2.50. Light wipes 4-5.15 Fetch-up 5.45
	20 Jan		16 men leave on demobilisation *DGE*	
	21 Jan		16 men leave on demobilisation. *DGE*	
	22 Jan		No men leave on demobilisation this day on tomorrow. Drawing out animals MSM n transport. Strength now 24977 B.S.M. AE JACOBS 519/785 S6992 Corporal F. HATELEY 140 5/35/a/893 *DGE*	9744 (h.i.147) Pte Orr 2.Q.R. Drew out animal transport
	23 Jan		40 horses champion for repatriation RUK left for M.E. reserves hover covered today, 14p. 1 10p.m. *DGE*	9 w/t wipers team report in from first by sea hopes RJ t
			1/3ᵗʰ and 13 men to hosp. *DGE*	
	24 Jan		16 men leave on demobilisation *DGE*	
	25 Jan		14 men leave on demobilisation. — 2 horses stolen from 28ᵈ/35 block. Kept officers' escorting, and horse is very high - fences by civilians. Civil police were in attendance. *DGE*	
	Sunday 26 Jan		No men left for demobilisation this day. Heavy part of snow during day and night. *DGE*	
	27 Jan		13 men left for demobilisation. *DGE*	
	28 Jan		Capt. L.S. LLOYD 28/35 and 12 O.R.s leave for demobilisation. *DGE*	
	29 Jan		12 men + 5 horses for repatriation to England for demobilisation Capt Foley *DGE*	

Army Form C. 2118.

WAR DIARY
INTELLIGENCE SUMMARY.
(Erase heading not required.) 9th Brigade R.H.A.

January 1919

Place	Date	Hour	Summary of Events and Information	Remarks and references to Appendices
CASTERO	30th Jan		No men demobilized today. 25 Z class horses arrived. 7th horsepower & Belgian horsemen at 9TH Rd Other Detagnments arrived. Lieut. T. BECKER, 18 F & 5 R.G.A. left for base H.R. (Simpson) for demobilization & proceed to S. Africa. DSO	
	31st Jan		No officers or men for demobilization today. Check put power at night.	

J.W. Martin
Colonel
Cmd. 9th Brigade R.H.A.

Confidential

War Diary
of
9th Brigade R.F.A.
from 1/3/19 to 28/9/19
(Volume 3)

Army Form C. 2118.

WAR DIARY
or
INTELLIGENCE SUMMARY.
(Erase heading not required.)

9th Brigade R.H.A.   February 1919.

Instructions regarding War Diaries and Intelligence Summaries are contained in F. S. Regs., Part II. and the Staff Manual respectively. Title pages will be prepared in manuscript.

Place	Date	Hour	Summary of Events and Information	Remarks and references to Appendices
CASTEAU	1st Feb.		21 men left for demobilization. They for service with 1st Division Army being forwarded and received in prepared who claimed them. SfAe	
	2nd Feb.		13 men left for demobilization. Under return from CRA 62nd Div. of (Regt) R R MYERS MC to posts K 9 B 4. Lt WARWICK & MEBB (gunner) attached from 52 TMB into this Bde and has posted K 9.23.6. and posts K 28.30.5. Sgt TRUEMAN 52 TMB is posted from 52 TMB K 29 Q.5. Ran as interpreter. A check up of T.M Batteries 9.52.D. SfAe	
	3rd Feb.		12 men left for demobilization. 3 ORs 19° & 5° OR 28° resubmits for points 1,2, 3 & 4 guns. 1 Sgt (Rent Fun) 28°B° engaged. The outcome at end of reinforcements in points 19°-12, 20° nd, 28°-8, 3/69 -6, and 6 unassigned pops. & 21 guns in points 20°. 5° . 28°. 1 . SfAe	
	4th Feb.		12 men left for demobilization. Some snow at night. SfAe	
	5th Feb.		No men for demobilization. R A Band played a MONS at the Theatre Royal. About E H HAYES MC joined Bde for course duties of Adjutant. Heavy fall of snow last night. SfAe	
	6th Feb.		No men for demobilization. Settling in more mild winter. This is because 7th Division in there & Cavalry Brigade New demobilization instructions are under review. 3 mm to expect about. Menes 13 KRSS 28° N referred to report KROUER for duty in Connection with test-officer horses. Lieut Farmer. SfAe	
	7th Feb.		Army news K.O. of 1919 received. No demobilisation on this issue. 4 men when 28°.B.5 released. SfAe	

Army Form C. 2118.

Instructions regarding War Diaries and Intelligence Summaries are contained in F.S. Regs., Part II. and the Staff Manual respectively. Title pages will be prepared in manuscript.

WAR DIARY
or
INTELLIGENCE SUMMARY.
(Erase heading not required.)

February 1919   9th Brigade RFA

Place	Date	Hour	Summary of Events and Information	Remarks and references to Appendices
CASTEAU	8/2/19		Severe frost at night – Bright crisp weather. Some Horses reported from leave.	9th Brigade Rets to 4/2/19 forwarded by 3.2. Trigoph of 6.30 am futures given
Sunday	9/2/19		Frost continues. 2nd Lt H.E. STANLEY proceeds to England on demobilisation. Range practice on B/69, one case and two charges.	
	10/2/19		1 man Do 235 recalled for turgina – One Coyl, on urgent industrial & one divm 28 Reg recalled for 4, 3, 3, and 2 years respectively. Attestation and forms for most approved. Frost continues & no proper exercise any temperature lower.	
	11/2/19		Snow and ices.	
	12/2/19		Frost continues. Also demobilisation rangs	
	13/2/19		Returns required by A.O. XIV of 9/19 re Officer volunteering for Germany & those not volunteering. Submitted. 30 Zebra horses and four Brigade for sale at MONS. Others drawing days chill contains.	
	14/2/19		18571 H SOWTER horseman 9th Brigade proceeded for demobilisation. M/88146 Staff Sgt Fitter R KATER authorised Military leave by Corp Comdr XXII Corps. Orders but one. Owing to necessity arising & horses & horses in substitution with Army gymkhana received, all horses marked A.X. or B.X, A.Y. or B.Y. are to be changed YM & fit for trading & appointed to R.U.K. H/g 30 Zebra horses sent for disposal & MONS 2/R on 20/2/19	
	15/2/19		Nothing to note.	
	16/2/19		Rain. Adoption of then precaution extra Capt G.H. STEWART. me Staff Capt C.A. 52nd Div. L.P. Division on term for an Stay Capt of Corps.	

Army Form C. 2118.

WAR DIARY
or
INTELLIGENCE SUMMARY.
(Erase heading not required.)

Instructions regarding War Diaries and Intelligence Summaries are contained in F. S. Regs., Part II. and the Staff Manual respectively. Title pages will be prepared in manuscript.

G.P. Bigouis Lt.Col   February 19

Place	Date	Hour	Summary of Events and Information	Remarks and references to Appendices
CASTEAU	19/2/19		Lt. R.H. SMITH G/OS proceeded to Concentration Camp for POW's conducting prisoners. 34 Z slave horses returned. POW's sent to MONS for disposal on 19/2/19. 7 off. 92 OR's Lt J.P. COUGHLAN G/OS attached to Bgde. Headqrs. Houplin left. 1355 UOS & J DUNEASE attached needed for 5 years. Major H.P. MORGAN 28th D.R. proceeded on leave to U.K. [sgd]	
	20/2/19			
	21/2/19		Major J HICKEY D/69 D's proceeded on leave to U.K. 200 Z horses (9 pm 19/2/19 6 4 party + 10 pm 26) sent to MONS for dispatch. 4 Y horses (4 for repatriation) ordered 8 m sent to MONS in view of rectifent Temps 3/2. these all came from 28/23m. [sgd]	
	22/2/19		Nothing known. [sgd]	
	23/2/19		2 horses 28/95 Rom Major Mayers Charger and 4. Y horses of same battery proceeded to MONS for repatriation to U.K. [sgd]	
	24/2/19		Orders to send 64 Z clean ammunition, mostly Miller, tomorrow to MONS for rail to ROUEN. Also 4 - Z horses D/69 D's also 4 th and K/ONCOMES for sale on 28/2/19. Dupont recruits. Conference with Dupont re "J Battery" this day. [sgd]	
Sunday	23/2/19		64 animals left for ROUEN - all Z class at 7 am. Lt Col H V OTTER received verbal warning this ordres are leaving directly him to proceed forth with to RPD for issue overseas. Orders received. That all Y horses - Excepting officers chargers - are to proceed to MONS in view of resent to happen. [sgd]	
	26/2/19		15 Y horses left for base parks under Lt. H.E.H. WINSHIP. Rom 27/69 M.S.Rom [sgd]	

Army Form C. 2118.

WAR DIARY
or
INTELLIGENCE SUMMARY.
(Erase heading not required.)

9th Div RFA   February 1919

Place	Date	Hour	Summary of Events and Information	Remarks and references to Appendices
CASTEAU	25/2/19		The men 28 Battery recruited for 4 years. JJSE	
"	26/2/19		4 horses (Riders) 57/69 and K Sergeants for sale. Also N J COTTER transferred from 527 Bty. 58/134 RFA prepared to leaving. A/B	
"	28.2.19		Lt Col H.J. COTTER left for England to report to W.O. (Authority 62 Divl Arty. A 131. 28/2/19) A/B	

A Roberts Maj. RFA.
OC 9 Bde RFA.

Vol 12

CONFIDENTIAL
WAR
DIARY
OF
9th BRIGADE RFA

From 1/3/19 To 31/3/19

(VOLUME B)

Army Form C. 2118.

WAR DIARY
or
INTELLIGENCE SUMMARY.
(Erase heading not required.)

9 Bde. R.F.A.   March 1919

Place	Date	Hour	Summary of Events and Information	Remarks and references to Appendices
CASTEAU	2		25 "Z" class animals to Mons for sale. A/B.	
"			24 G.P. WEBB posted to 56 Bde R.F.A. A/B.	
"	4		19 "Z" class mules to FORGES for sale. A/B.	
"	6		60 Z mules to Mons for sale. A/B.	
"	10		Posting of officers:—	
			Major BLOCK D.S.O. To 20 Bty and remain temporarily in command of 9 Bde.	
			A/" PRINGLE To remain temporarily in command of 20 Bty	
			Major LUND from A/147 Bty. To command 19 Bty	
			Lieut BROWN from A/560 Bty. To D/69 Bty	
			Lieut WINSHIP " D/69 " A/56 "	
			A/Capt MEABURN " 19 Bty To 28 Bty	
			A/ " MURAS " 28 " " 282nd A/Bty. E/H.Q.	
	12		Capt. WOOD To 527 Bty. Major LUND D.S.O. has just joined E/H.Q.	
	13		Lt Smith rejoined from conducting officer E/H.Q.	
	14		8 y mares to MONS.	
	15		70 x mules to 77 Army Bde + 45 Divn E/H.S.	
	17		24 Z horses to BOULOGNE E/H.	
	16		Capt URIE attached from 147 Army Bde. E/H.	

WAR DIARY or INTELLIGENCE SUMMARY.

Army Form C. 2118.

9 Bde R.F.A.

March 1919

Place	Date	Hour	Summary of Events and Information	Remarks and references to Appendices
CATEAU	19.		All Ammunition returned to dump at MONS.	A/B
"	20.		H.Q. 19, 20 & 28 Batteries marched to billets in SOIGNIES, D/Bty remaining at THIEUSIS. H.Q. at 212 rue Gregoire Wincqz.	A/B
SOIGNIES	21.		Officers for Cadre B, authority 52 D.A. M.S.C. 309 d/- 21.3.19	
			H.Q. { Maj A. BLOCK. D.S.O. Lieut & Capt. E.H. GAGE M.S. } 19 Bty { Maj. O.M. LUND. D.S.O. Lieut & Capt R.E. URIE (posted from 149 Bde) 2Lt H.E. SIMS (" " ") }	
			20 Bty { Lt a/Maj. H.C. WATT-PRINGLE. Lt a/Capt. E.C.H. ALBAN Lt N.A. WOOLLACOTT. } 28 Bty { Maj. H.T. MORGAN 2Lt a/Capt M. MEABURN 2Lt J. LYDDON }	
			D/Bty Bty { Maj. J. HICKEY Lt C.W.C. BROWN 2Lt A. ANDERSON }	
"	23.		Posted from 52 Bde R.T.A. - O.Rs 31 horses 100 " " 14 " " " 68 " " " 41 " " " " " 10 52 D.A.C.	A/B

Army Form C. 2118.

WAR DIARY
or
INTELLIGENCE SUMMARY. 9 B.L. R.F.A

(Erase heading not required.)

March 1919

Place	Date	Hour	Summary of Events and Information	Remarks and references to Appendices
SOIGNIES	28		2/Lt R.W. SMITH ~~hostpital~~ left for demobilization /a/B	
"	31		26 O.R. posted from 56 Bde R.F.A /a/-	
			Maj O.M. LUND D.S.O. left to report to W.O /a/-	

(signed) Blank Maj R.F.A
O.C. 9 B.L. R.F.A

CONFIDENTIAL 9B 13

WAR DIARY

OF

9TH BRIGADE R.F.A.

From 1/4/19 to 30/4/19

(VOLUME 4)

INTELLIGENCE SUMMARY. 9 Bde R.F.A.

April 1919

Instructions regarding War Diaries and Intelligence Summaries are contained in F.S. Regs., Part II and the Staff Manual respectively. Title pages will be prepared in manuscript.

(Erase heading not required.)

Place	Date	Hour	Summary of Events and Information	Remarks and references to Appendices
SOIGNIES	10		All animals left for U.K. in charge of Maj. MORGAN. M.C. /a/b	
"	11		a Capt (Actg) E.C.H. ALBAN + 20 O.R. (untrainable men) left, 1 on posting to 2d Army in Germany /a/b	
"	12		32 O.R. posted to 58 Bde R.F.A.	
			38 O.R. " " 147 " "	
			47 O.R. " " D.A.C. /a/b	
"	13		3 shoeing smiths " 58 Bde "	
			2 " " 147 " "	
			7 " " D.A.C. /a/b	
			Division commenced to entrain for U.K. h.C.O.s surplus to establishmt A left for demobilization.	
"	27.		2Lt ANDERSON posted to RHINE.	
"	28.			
"	30		2Lt COLLETT posted to D.A.C.	

(Signed) W Welsh Maj RFA
OC 9 Bde RFA

www.ingramcontent.com/pod-product-compliance
Lightning Source LLC
Chambersburg PA
CBHW081441160426
43193CB00013B/2345